OUTDOOR LIFE

THE SPORTSMAN'S AUTHORITY SINCE 1898 ®

Hunting Big Game

IN NORTH AMERICA

Outdoor Life's EXPERTS REVEAL
THEIR SECRETS FOR TAKING
TROPHY ANTLERED, HORNED &
DANGEROUS GAME

CREATIVE
PUBLISHING
international

MINNETONKA, MINNESOTA

Creative Publishing international, Inc.
5900 Green Oak Drive
Minnetonka, MN 55343
1-800-328-3895

President/CEO: David D. Murphy
Vice President/Editorial: Patricia K. Jacobsen
Vice President/Retail Sales & Marketing: Richard M. Miller

HUNTING BIG GAME IN NORTH AMERICA

Executive Editor, Outdoor Group: Don Oster
Editorial Director and Project Leader: David R. Maas
Managing Editor: Jill Anderson
Project Manager: Tracy Stanley
Creative Director: Brad Springer
Photo Researcher: Angela Hartwell
Copy Editor: Shannon Zemlicka
Director, Production Services: Kim Gerber
Production Manager: Helga Thielen
Production Staff: Laura Hokkanen, Kay Swanson

Contributing Photographers: Chuck Adams, Jack Atcheson, Jr., Judd Cooney,
Rita Groszmann, Michael Hanback, Donald M. Jones, Mark Kayser, Bill Lea,
Stephen W. Maas, Bill Marchel, Robert McCaw, Bob McNally, Michael Pearce,
Bob Robb, Tom Walker, Lyle Willmarth, Jim Zumbo

Contributing Illustrators: Ken Laager, Leon Parson

Cover Illustrator: cover illustration of "Storm's End" by Larry Zach, Zach Wildlife Art,
tel: 515-964-1570

Printed on American paper by: R. R. Donnelley & Sons Co.

10 9 8 7 6 5 4 3 2 1

Library of Congress Cataloging-in-Publication Data

Hunting big game in North America.
    p. cm.
"Outdoor Life."
  ISBN 0-86573-123-3 (softcover)
  1. Hunting--North America. 2. Big game hunting--North America.
  I. Creative Publishing International.
  SK40 .H862 2000
  799.2'6'097--dc21
                                                    00-022718

Table of Contents

Introduction

The book you're about to read contains, without a doubt, the finest collection of big-game hunting articles and tales ever produced. Each chapter was carefully selected from past issues of *Outdoor Life* magazine, considered to be the authoritative publication on big-game hunting in North America.

As one who has been writing for *Outdoor Life* since 1964, I'm perhaps a bit biased in extolling the virtues of these writers and articles. But you be the judge, and I'll wager that you won't be able to put this book down until the last page is read.

If you're a deer hunter, no matter where you live or how you hunt, you'll enjoy the articles that tell how to outwit your next deer, whether it's a whitetail, blacktail, or muley. If you're planning your first elk hunt, or are a veteran with plenty of seasons under your belt, you'll likewise see stories offering solid advice to help you line up your sights on an elusive bull. And if you think you must pay a fortune to find the trophy bull of your dreams, read how Merwin Martin took one of the biggest bulls of the last century on public land a short distance from a road. Just about every big-game species hunted in the lower 48 is included, and the Far North is represented too, with tales about caribou, moose, and grizzlies.

If adventure is your game, you'll find plenty of it here, such as the tale, "Death Came Running – Twice," where the author was attacked and almost killed by a rampaging grizzly. Another bear story is recounted by veteran Montana outdoorsman Bill McRae as he relates more chilling encounters. And who can resist reading Russell Annabel, perhaps the champion tale-spinner of all time, as he tells of his always-captivating Alaskan adventures.

So sit back in your most comfortable chair and escape with these wonderful stories. Be prepared to be informed as well as entertained, whether you hunt in the back forty or around the continent. This book has it all.

Jim Zumbo, Hunting Editor, Outdoor Life

ANTLERED
GAME

ANTLERED GAME

Walk Up a Buck

BY GARY CLANCY

Slowly stillhunting for whitetails has provided me with some of my biggest bucks and some of my most memorable moments afield.

Snow had fallen from the black, November sky during most of the night. By the time the four of us had wolfed down a quick breakfast, struggled into layers of wool clothing and exited the cramped quarters of the pickup camper, the last few sloppy flakes spattered against our faces.

Sitting on stand was like being stuffed inside a box of wet cotton balls. The snow clung to every branch, bush and twig, transforming the normally dull-brown November hardwoods into an unbroken world of surgical white. The world seemed to be frozen that morning; nothing moved. Even the nervous, always active chickadees and nuthatches were conspicuous by their absence. It was as if every living creature was being held prisoner by this suddenly stark white world. By 9 a.m., I had tired of staring at the nothingness and climbed down from my tree to try my hand at stillhunting.

This was not my first attempt at stillhunting. Several times during the past few seasons I had attempted to sneak along the ridges hoping to surprise a deer. Oh, I had surprised them, but all I ever saw was a waving white tail flipping in the distance. But maybe this time . . . .

WITH SOFT SNOW covering the ground, stillhunting is a great way to slip up on unsuspecting whitetails.

For two hours I had been sneaking through the leg-thick aspens cloaking the ridge. Move a few steps, stop, look, kneel to peer beneath the snow-laden underbrush, slowly stand, take a few more steps and do it all again. So far I had seen a ruffed grouse and a gray squirrel, both appearing huge against the unbroken curtain of white. But then, when I knelt in the wet snow for the umpteenth time, something out of place caught my eye. There were four slender, brown saplings in a sea of endless white, and one of the saplings had moved. The deer was only 10 yards away, but try as I might, all I could see were the legs and patches of cream-colored belly. Then all four legs began to piston. The deer was coming my way. I stayed on my knees and when the deer, a heavy-bodied, thick-necked five-point buck was 11 feet away, I took him. My deer hunting has not been the same since.

On that snowy Minnesota morning 20 years ago, I proved to myself that stillhunting was not beyond the scope of my capabilities. During the two decades that have passed since that day, I have successfully stillhunted whitetail deer in a dozen states while carrying rifle, shotgun, muzzleloader or bowhunting gear. Yet, even after all those years, each time I go out, I learn something about myself, about deer or about some of the intricacies of stillhunting that I did not know before. Stillhunting is the most demanding, exciting and satisfying method there is for hunting the whitetail.

Before we start, these are the questions we need answers for: Who can stillhunt? Why would I want to stillhunt? What do I need to be a good stillhunter? When is the best time to stillhunt? Where should I stillhunt? How do I stillhunt?

Who Can Stillhunt?

Anyone can be a stillhunter. You do not need Daniel Boone's blood coursing through your veins. It matters not whether you live in the country or the city. The ability to slip undetected within range of whitetail deer is not something some hunters are born with and others are not. Rather, it is a skill acquired and honed through practice. Doing it whenever you hunt is the only way to get better.

Why Would I Want to Stillhunt?

Not everyone does want to stillhunt. Not everyone should. If you are perfectly happy with your present hunting strategy, then my advice is to stick with it. However, if you, like me, sometimes find yourself bored while sitting on stand, or tired of making drives, and wish that there was some way you could actively hunt whitetail deer without involving other hunters, then stillhunting is the perfect remedy. Stillhunting is great fun.

Although stillhunting is often looked upon as a technique with a very low hunter-success rate, I disagree with that assessment. Under the right conditions, stillhunting can be the most effective hunting method you can employ. That includes driving.

What Do I Need to Be a Good Stillhunter?

The most important ingredient of stillhunting success cannot be purchased at your favorite sporting-goods store. It's patience. Patience is imperative to success when stillhunting. Impatient hunters move too fast, at the wrong times and in the wrong places. They see bits and pieces of escaping deer and soon write off stillhunting as a waste of time. Impatient hunters give up on stillhunting too easily. Becoming an accomplished stillhunter takes practice, time in the woods, trial and error and then learning from your experiences. Most hunters are not willing to make that kind of an investment.

If you are determined to be a stillhunter, then here is the equipment that will help you attain that goal.

No matter how accomplished you become at stillhunting, there are always going to be instances that call for fast reactions and quick shooting. It is vital that you be intimately familiar with your firearm or bow. You can kiss that buck goodbye if during that split second when he bursts from his bed on the other side of a windfall, giving you but one fleeting moment to make the shot, you fumble for the safety or the arrow, catch the butt in your armpit or have to adjust your head on the stock to line up the sights.

Quiet is the key word when selecting clothing for stillhunting. Stick with wool, fleece and soft cotton. When choosing a garment for still-hunting, give it this test. Hold the article of clothing at arm's length and drag your fingernails across the fabric. If you can hear it, it is too noisy for stillhunting.

Boots should have soft, pliable soles. My favorite is the old standby L.L. Bean hunting boot with leather uppers and rubber bottoms and soles.

Binoculars are a must. The old advice to buy the best pair you can afford is legitimate. I would add, though, that I would rather hunt with the cheapest binoculars made than hunt without them at all. I have used an inexpensive pair of Bushnell 7X25 compacts with good results for years.

Many hunters use binoculars to help them positively identify suspicious objects and movements. That is fine, but a stillhunter needs to use binoculars so that he can pick apart every bit of cover before advancing, whether he has spotted anything with the naked eye or not. I can't begin to count all of the deer I have seen first through the glasses. Nor do I wish to recall all of the deer I have spooked because I managed to convince myself once again that scanning the area ahead of me with the unaided eye was sufficient.

When Is the Best Time to Stillhunt?

Unfortunately, most would-be stillhunters attempt to stillhunt at the worst possible times. See if this scenario sounds familiar.

It is opening day of the firearms deer season. You have been in your stand since before first light, filled with all of the anticipation and confidence inherent to opening mornings everywhere. But after a few hours, you have not seen a deer from your carefully chosen stand. You just know that everyone else has seen deer—judging from the number of shots you have heard, most hunters are probably already back in camp with their deer hanging from meat poles. Disgusted, you climb down from your stand and begin to "stillhunt" your way up the valley. The leaves are dry and the going is noisy, but your heart really isn't in it anyway so you continue to plod on, stopping occasionally to lazily scan the cover ahead for deer that you know are not there. Halfway up the valley, a buck breaks from cover ahead of you. Startled, you fail to react quickly enough, and the buck disappears. A moment later a shot sounds from the direction in which the buck ran. When you arrive on the scene, a young hunter is dressing out a dandy eight-pointer.

"He just came scooting down that hill as if something had spooked him," the excited hunter tells you. "Funny thing is, I was ready to climb down from my stand an hour ago. Sure glad I stuck it out."

If that little scene sounds familiar, join the crowd—that is how most of us attempt to stillhunt. We tend to look upon stillhunting as a diversion between morning and evening stints on stand. What we are really doing is simply walking in the woods, not stillhunting.

Successful stillhunters know when they can—and just as importantly know when they cannot—effectively stillhunt. Here are the criteria I use to make that decision.

Although most discussions on stillhunting center around the weather conditions that enable hunters to stillhunt effectively, my first consideration is hunting pressure. If hunting pressure is significant, as it nearly always is during the first few days of the season, stillhunting is a poor choice. Staying put on stand and letting the activities of other hunters move deer past your position is a much better option.

However, even in states where hordes of hunters are afield on the opening weekend of the firearms season, the crowds thin out as the season progresses and stillhunting becomes a viable option.

It is impossible to stillhunt effectively if conditions are such that the deer are going to easily detect you before you are aware of their presence. Attempting to stillhunt on tinder-dry forest duff on a calm day is a fool's mission. Crusted snow is another condition that eliminates stillhunting as an option. Rain, wet snow, heavy dew and melted frost all make the forest floor a quiet carpet.

On windy days, stillhunting is possible on the noisiest footing. It takes a breeze of at least 15 mph to whisk away the crunch of your footsteps. Always hunt either crosswind or into the wind. Deer, though, know that their senses are impaired on windy days so they are even jumpier than normal. Take care to move slower than usual when stillhunting on windy days.

Wind-whipped branches and brush also make detecting deer by movement difficult, so let those binoculars help you look for the colors, shapes and angles of the different parts of a whitetail's body. The white along the belly, tail, inside of the legs, throat patch, inside of the ears and face markings show up well against the backgrounds of an autumn forest. When there is snow on the ground, the white on a deer becomes difficult to detect, but often the black shine of a buck's nose, the glint of light from a dark eye, the black V of the tail or the dark brown stain of a rutting buck's tarsal glands stand out well against the white background. The distinct angle of a cocked leg, the slope of a delicate neck, the oval shape of a bedded deer, the rounded form of a deer's rump and the horizontal plane of a standing buck's belly and back are all shapes and angles that will help you pick him out from the surrounding collage of deadfalls, branches, stumps and rocks.

My own stillhunting success escalated dramatically when I broke from the tradition of stillhunting between the dawn and dusk vigils on stand and, instead, used these nearly sacred sitting hours for stillhunting. Slowly prowling through the edge cover deer use most during these hours has provided me with some of my most memorable moments afield. Deer that are moving are much easier to detect than deer that have bedded down. Stillhunting early and late in the day gives me the opportunity to intercept deer between feeding and bedding sites, or especially when the deer are keying on browse and mast, to hunt the feeding area itself. The ultimate in stillhunting occurs when the deer are pigging out on acorns, a whitetail favorite nationwide. When this happens, slowly prowling the oak ridges is the most exciting form of whitetail hunting I know.

A couple of years ago while on an early December hunt with Bill Jordan, the hard-hunting head honcho of Realtree Camouflage, we found the abundant Georgia whitetails keying on fallen acorns and hickory nuts. Rain fell for most of the four days I prowled those ridges, but I didn't mind at all. The rain made the footing silent, and the abundant deer, hungrily snuffling through the leaves for the high-protein nuts, made me all but oblivious to the cold rain. I saw more than 30 deer each day I hunted, killed a nice nine-pointer and missed an even bigger buck. Three of my friends were hunting from stands during the same period and were seeing only a third of the deer that I was seeing.

Where Should I Stillhunt?

You can stillhunt anywhere deer are found, but your odds of getting within range of an unsuspecting whitetail are greatest if you seek out either of two types of habitat and land configuration for stillhunting. One is open timber, the other is hill country.

Open timber does not refer to pastured woodlots or the neatly manicured stands of pine common to timber company land. My definition of open timber is anywhere you stand a reasonable chance of seeing deer at 100 yards or farther. The odds of deer detecting you before you are aware of their presence escalate as that distance decreases. Attempting to stillhunt in extremely heavy cover such as brier patches, cattail marshes, alder runs and overgrown cedar swamps is a waste of energy.

Invariably, I have better stillhunting results in hill country than on flat ground. The reason for the big difference in my success on these two types of terrain is because deer can see you at a greater distance on flat ground than in rolling hills. By using the contour of the land to mask my approach, I have often stillhunted to within point-blank range of deer in hill country. Such close-range encounters are rare on flat land.

One of my favorite techniques when hunting in the hills is to pussyfoot my way along a ridge that runs dead into the wind. I move just below the crest along one side of the ridge for 50 to 100 yards, and then, crouching low to skyline myself as little as possible, I slip over to the opposite side. Many times, just as I crest the ridge I will spot deer just below me. I call the technique "snaking the ridge," and it is one of the deadliest forms of stillhunting you can use when conditions for its use are favorable.

How Should I Stillhunt?

Trying to instruct someone on how to stillhunt is like trying to explain to someone how to make love—there are some things you just need to learn as you go. However, here are four tips that will get you started:

•Force yourself to slow down. The world we live in puts a premium on speed. Rush here, hurry there, grab a bite on the run, dash off to work, make like O.J. to catch that plane. Our everyday lives are consumed by the desire to do more and to do it faster. Stillhunting goes against that notion. Most hunters who are unsuccessful at stillhunting are simply not able to throttle down their internal engines to the idle speed best suited to stillhunting. I think that explains why I always see fewer flags and more shootable deer when stillhunting as the season progresses. During the early days of the season I am still locked into that hurry-hurry mode, and the abundance of white flags mocking me in the distance reflects my condition. As the season progresses, though, and I become more in tune with the slower flow of life in the woods, I am able to sneak up on increasing numbers of deer that are unaware of my presence.

•Limit body motion. Most of us tend to swagger, sway and swing our arms when we walk down the street. All that extra motion in the woods will make you an easy mark for the whitetails' incredible ability to detect movement. Only your legs should be in motion when you take a step.

•When walking, put your foot down either heel or toe first, whichever is most comfortable for you, and then let the rest of the foot roll slowly into place. By doing this you will be able to feel most sticks beneath your feet before they crack.

• Pre-plan your next series of steps each time you stop. Look ahead 20 to 30 feet (you should never move farther than that between stops) and plan your route. Take advantage of game trails, old roads, creek beds, fallen trees, patches of bare earth and anything else that will

PLAN YOUR STOPS next to trees or other types of cover to break up your outline.

help you move as quietly as possible. Plan detours around patches of crusty snow, thick beds of sun-dried leaves, heavy brush and deadfalls. Then purposefully plan each stop next to a tree, deadfall or bush; this will break up your outline and provide a steady rest for your rifle if a shot presents itself.

If you ever visit my home, you may notice a shoulder mount of a whitetail buck in the corner of my den. There is nothing extraordinary about the 10-point rack. But each time I look at the mount of that not-so-big 10-point, I remember the way the woods smelled on that rainy November morning, I can hear again the patter of the raindrops on already soggy leaves, I feel again his eyes on mine when he caught me in midstride, and the rush of relief I felt when he finally put his head down and went back to the business of finding an acorn beneath the sopping forest duff.

I took him by stillhunting, and to me, that—more than sheer size—makes him a trophy.

Outdoor Life, September 1991

Deer Drives That Work

BY JIM ZUMBO

I've seen numerous deer drives fail to push out any good bucks. But there have been others that have worked to perfection.

My vantage point was perfect. From the granite ridgetop, I could look down into the hardwood forest and see practically everything that moved. Leaves were already claimed by autumn's demands, offering good visibility through the naked branches.

I wasn't in a good shooting position for the whitetails that lived in the woods around me, because the forest floor below was much too far for a shot. However, I had a bird's-eye view of a scenario that was about to unfold. Eight hunters were positioned to make a drive; I could see practically all of their drive area.

Four hunters were driving, four were standing. In typical fashion, the standers covered the flanks and the end of the area being driven.

I watched six deer bounce out of their beds as the hunt began. Four were does, one a small buck, the other a good eight-point buck. The deer moved ahead of the hunters, but were reluctant to leave the forest.

As the drivers walked, they shouted and whacked trees with branches. Finally, three does raced out across one of the flanks and into a field. The remaining doe and the small buck minced along lightly, refusing to break cover. They stayed in the forest, slipping back between the drivers and finally exiting the drive area from where the drivers first began. The big buck never moved more than 50 yards during the drive. He eased about, always remaining in the scattered laurel patches. When a driver passed close to the buck, the deer stood silently, allowing the hunter to approach within 10 yards. The man never saw the buck.

I recognized the hunters through my binoculars and chatted with them a couple of hours later. They told me that they'd seen only a few does during a drive they made.

They complained of too many hunters and said that the seasons were too long. They blamed the state game department for the lack of bucks and shook their heads in disgust.

Whitetails have a way of causing consternation during deer drives. More often than not, most bucks escape the strategy, many of them never seen by drivers and standers.

On paper, a deer drive appears to be an almost perfect, foolproof strategy. It seems to be a simple maneuver. You merely surround a prescribed spot with hunters, have another bunch of hunters walk through to rout out the deer, and hopefully the standers can get an opportunity for a shot as the deer emerge.

Off paper and in the field, however, it's a different story. Deer don't follow the rules. They behave like deer rather than subjects that should conform to our expectations.

Deer driving strategies can be complex or simple, depending on the creativity of the hunters who design them. I know a bunch of men who tried drives with helium-filled balloons and portable radios positioned at various points around the drive fringes. The idea was to keep deer moving toward certain exit points watched by standers. Every now and then a deer followed the intended route; most often they didn't.

A veteran whitetail hunter once told me his opinion, which pretty much sums up deer driving: "You can't make a deer go where you want it to go. They'll go where they feel like it, and a lot of the time they don't go anywhere. They stay put."

That doesn't mean that drives are worthless maneuvers. They do indeed work much of the time and are an effective means of seeing deer. For them to work, however, you must understand deer behavior. Although it's possible to get lucky and take a good deer during drives, many of the bigger bucks are killed by hunters who know something about the quarry.

My first whitetail buck, taken about 30 years ago, was a result of a drive. It wasn't a simple happenstance either; the deer showed because my mentor had the drive area figured out perfectly.

He and a companion walked a rocky ridge that deer frequently used as a bedding area. I was positioned where I could see a well-used trail coming off the ridge and into a hemlock thicket. My pal was placed near another trail that fell away from the other side of the ridge and into a honeysuckle tangle.

My friend and I were told to listen for a crow cawing. We were to get ready if we heard it, because the drivers were signaling that deer were coming our way.

Twenty minutes after the drive began, I heard a crow from up on the ridge, and I positioned my rifle. Presently a forkhorn buck ran down the precise trail I was watching. A case of buck fever almost cost me the deer, but I managed to compose myself, taking the deer before it entered the safety of the hemlocks.

Because the drive worked exactly according to plan, I figured that there was nothing to whitetail hunting. My friend who engineered the drive, however, set me straight.

"You were at the right spot at the right time," he said. "The stand you were on doesn't produce a buck during every drive. There are several trails off the ridge; deer can use any of them. The one you watched is one of the primary exit routes."

He was right. Since that hunt, I've been involved in lots of deer drives. None have worked as perfectly as my first.

An interesting perception about drives persists. Many hunters believe that standers are in the best position. Straws are often drawn—the winners get to be standers; the losers are the drivers.

During my early deer hunting years, I used to think that standers would see most of the animals, but now I've reversed my opinion. Too many times, I've seen far more deer while driving than the standers have seen.

Plenty of drives have ended with the frustrated driver saying to the stander, "Didn't that buck run by you? Saw him twice in that jungle, and I thought he was headed your way." The stander never saw the buck because it either didn't come out at all or slipped by unseen through the perimeter of the drive area.

Given my choice, I'll be a driver every time, provided the ground rules allow the driver to shoot. If they don't, I'll flip a coin along with the rest of the crowd. During some drives, only the standers shoot because of safety reasons. When that's done, the drivers sometimes make noise during the drive so that the standers know where they are. The standers should know where the other standers are, too.

That brings up an important point. Because hunters are concentrated in one area during a drive, and because they usually can't see each other, safety must be a priority. Some states, in fact, strictly regulate deer drives because of the possibility of accidents.

One way to eliminate much guesswork in keeping your companions located is to take a standing position from atop a big rock, hill or a tree. Your elevated vantage point will help you see the quarry more easily, along with other hunters.

Two types of drives are possible: silent and noisy. The latter type includes all sorts of shenanigans from whacking trees and brush with a stick, to beating on a drum, banging on a metal pot, singing, shouting, barking like a dog and so on. The idea is to spook deer from their beds toward the standers.

Aside from being safer (because drivers pinpoint their positions), I don't much care for a noisy drive. Just as standers can locate the drivers, so can the deer. Rather than being terrified of the loud sounds and bounding off wildly, deer know precisely where the drivers are, and they use that knowledge to their advantage. A wise buck is apt to stay bedded, stand in a thicket or sneak around, consistently avoiding the people who are walking about.

The silent driver, on the other hand, slips around quietly, unnerving deer because of his secretive wanderings. You can bet that deer know the hunter is around, but animals are often confused because the driver never offers a continuous clue as to his whereabouts. When that occurs, deer are more likely to leave the area rather than take their chances within.

Smart drivers never walk a straight line. They zigzag across cover, entering every thicket and pocket of underbrush, or at least tossing in a rock or heavy branch. Wary deer will often allow you to approach within a couple of yards before flushing.

I'll always remember a drive in Montana several years ago. A companion walked adjacent to a pile of brush no bigger than my pickup truck. He was about to walk by, but thought better of it and threw a rock in. To our amazement, a nine-point whitetail buck (Eastern count) jumped out and ran straight to a stander who promptly lowered the boom and claimed the deer.

Select a small area to drive, preferably between 2 and 50 acres. To put that into perspective, consider that one square mile is 640 acres. Although you never have precise control over deer movements, you'll have practically none in a huge area and a lot more in a smaller one.

Don't always place standers in places that offer a 360° view of a large open area, such as a field, meadow or sparsely scattered forest. If a big buck is going to exit the drive area at all, you can bet he'll depart through a narrow finger of thick brush or a timbered corridor. Practically every good buck I've taken as a stander on a drive tried to get out via a dense thicket. Furthermore, most bucks have an escape spot they're headed to. Put standers between the drive area and places where deer will seek security, such as swamps, dense evergreen stands and other thick spots.

Here's a solution to spot deer that run back through the line of drivers. Few hunters try it because it seems silly. Place a stander at the beginning of the drive, remaining there until the drive is complete. Also, place some standers at early flank positions, rather than at the end of the drive. I've seen situations where more deer exited the drive area closer to where it started than where it ended.

If you're a driver, take your time. Walk slowly, erratically, and investigate every pocket of brush. Your job is to rout deer and run them past your pals who are waiting. Be extra careful if you're a shooter because of the safety factor.

Many hunters don't realize that wind direction is often the primary reason a drive fails. If you're a stander and the wind is at your back, blowing your scent into the drive area, a dozen bulldozers won't run a smart buck by you. A solution is to change the direction of the drive or at least to wear a masking or cover scent.

Be absolutely silent if you're a stander. Remember that you're set up to perpetrate an ambush. Deer must be unaware that you're in the area.

When your group approaches the drive area, sneak up to it quietly. Have a specific plan in mind. Don't shout for Harry to sit next to the big white oak tree or holler to Sam to watch the old apple orchard. You want to catch the quarry unaware and not spook them off beforehand.

Putting on a successful drive is a whole lot more than just setting a bunch of hunters around a thicket and walking people through it. Use common sense, but be innovative. By not conforming to the schemes used by other hunters, you'll have a better chance of seeing more deer.

Remember the advice that driven deer will go where they want to go. It's up to you to figure out where that is.

Outdoor Life, October 1991

Dark Secrets

BY CHARLES J. ALSHEIMER

*Is a nocturnal buck
impossible to bag?
Not if you hold the
keys to hunting in his
daytime bedroom.*

Deer hunters are an interesting lot. No two will agree on where the best whitetail hunting exists today. Some rave about Anticosti Island, others say Texas is the place to go, while still others swear by Saskatchewan and its big-racked bucks.

But all will agree on one thing about whitetails: The toughest, most challenging of the species are most certainly nocturnal bucks.

Next to a natural disaster, nothing changes whitetail behavior quite like humans entering a deer's domain. Left to themselves for nine months of the year, deer roam their world openly, grazing and watering by day. But once the first signs of autumn arrive and hunters invade their woods, deer grow more wary. As October drifts toward November and the rut, deer become increasingly nocturnal.

For the most part, bucks—and mature bucks in particular—seldom abandon their home range when pressured by man. Instead, they change their lifestyle. Where do they go? Study after study has shown that mature bucks exhibit a strong preference for familiar terrain, a core area unaltered by intense hunting pressure. They respond to hunting pressure by hiding and decreasing daytime activity rather than utilizing unfamiliar areas. They become increasingly wary, inactive and nocturnal.

Each year, I'm able to pursue whitetails in parts of North America where hunting pressure is minimal, but the bulk of my deer hunting takes place in the Northeast, where pressure is intense. And I learned a long time ago that when humans take to the woods in large numbers, whitetails change their movement patterns. I've also learned that to consistently bag nice-racked bucks, learning to hunt nocturnal animals is essential.

A mature whitetail buck is the ultimate survival machine . . . bar none. By the time he's reached 3.5 years of age all of the survival tricks he needs are second nature. He knows where to bed, where to escape, and he's familiar with every inch of his home range. He also knows that the woods are quieter and smell safer during the cover of darkness. And as a result, most of his movement takes place under the stars. I'm a believer that some bucks are nearly impossible to hunt because of their nocturnal habits. But even the wariest bucks make mistakes when the rut approaches.

Ten years ago we had a dandy 10-point roaming our farm throughout the summer and early autumn months. It was not uncommon to see him in hayfields at the edge of day, but once October and small-game hunting pressure arrived he disappeared. I never saw him in daylight during the hunting season, but I was able to observe him at night with the use of a light, which is legal in New York when firearms are not present. This nocturnal buck taught me that normally productive strategies such as hunting food sources and transition zones where deer move between feeding and bedding areas lost a great deal of their effectiveness once hunting pressure mounted. I also realized that if I wanted to hunt and kill a buck of his caliber I'd have to change the way I hunted.

The strategies I've adopted have as their basis finding where mature bucks spend their daylight hours—prime bedding areas. Nearly 30 years of experience have taught me that the biggest bucks seek out the thickest cover when hunting pressure increases. The thicker the cover, the better they like it.

Topo maps and aerial photos taken after leaves have fallen can give a general idea where bedding areas might be located. Darker shades on aerial photos, for example, when they coincide with steep elevation lines on a topo map of the region, are one indicator of likely bedding areas. Whitetails love to bed just over ridges with the wind at their back. Such a position enables them to scan a good distance downwind and smell danger in the direction they cannot see. These setups also give them multiple escape routes up or down the slope.

When heading into the woods, ask yourself this question: "If I were a deer, where would I hide?" Often, you'll come across an area that just says "bedding area." If it's thick, has quick escape options and water and food are nearby, it's a prime candidate. When you see such a place, you'll know it.

Once deer season ends I take to the woods to seek out new bedding areas and check on known ones, and I try to determine from them which bucks survived the season. Such forays allow me to see how deer escape when jumped from their beds. The number of deer jumped in a prospective zone helps determine what possibilities it holds for the following season, and track sizes indicate the quality of the animals I'm dealing with. If a track is more than 3½ inches long and 2 inches wide, a nice-size deer is in the area.

If snow is on the ground when I'm scouting, I circle a bedding area to determine where deer are entering and exiting the thick cover. Locating access routes goes a long way toward planning hunting strategy come fall.

Once the snow has melted in the spring I return to bedding areas and look for nearby rutting sign from the past fall—rubs, scrapes and overhanging licking branches. When hunting pressure forces a buck into nocturnal movement he'll scrape, rub and breed in the confines of his bedding area. It's important to note that bucks will use a favorite scrape throughout the year. Though they won't paw the ground year-round, they will work the overhanging licking branch continually. By periodically clearing leaves from below active licking branches I'm able to determine the size of the deer working the scrape by its tracks.

In the early summer, I prepare a core area for the fall's hunt by making two or three narrow entrance trails to a stand location near a bedding area. Multiple trails allow me to change my entrance and exit patterns each time I enter the buck's bedroom. If only one trail is used a buck will quickly pick up your habits and move. The trick is to keep the area as natural and thick as possible while enabling quiet access.

Because permanent stands are a dead giveaway to a mature buck, I never erect one when hunting a nocturnal animal. Rather, I use a portable stand. At least two weeks prior to hunting, I set up my stand in a tree that will break up my outline.

The key to hunting nocturnal bucks is to scout and stalk them without their knowledge of your presence. As much as possible, scout a buck's core area from afar with binoculars or a spotting scope so that the area won't be disturbed. It's best not to frequent the area once autumn arrives, but if you do venture into a buck's core region, mask your scent with a good cover-up and be as quiet as possible. This point is critical.

Once the groundwork is done and the hunt is on, a buck's bedding area should be treated with heightened caution. I'm careful not to overhunt a buck's sanctuary, but once on stand I'm prepared to stay all day. Over the years I've had numerous chances to kill bucks between 10 a.m. and 2 p.m., and high noon is an excellent time to have Mr. Big show up. One example occurred during my 1990 season.

Hunting pressure had been fairly intense for the first two weeks of New York's gun season. So, on the second Saturday I decided to hunt a portable stand in the thickest cover I knew, a hemlock-covered bench on a steep hillside.

Through the morning no shots were fired close by, though I knew hunters were in the area. Except for an early morning sighting of a doe and two fawns, only chickadees and scurrying gray squirrels kept me company. My mind drifted as the noon whistle blew in the village five miles away. The woods were silent, and I knew that most hunters were probably eating sandwiches and sipping coffee in the local diner.

Just then I heard a branch snap to my left, followed by the gentle rustling of leaves. I strained to see, hoping the disturbance was more than a mere raucous squirrel, but I couldn't make out what it was through the trees. The sound grew louder as its maker approached.

From behind a small hemlock a fawn stepped into view, followed by a second. When the first fawn looked back over its shoulder I readied my gun. Both scampered off through the hemlocks as an eight-point walked into view.

Sensing he was going to follow, I picked out an opening in the brush and fired the 12-gauge when he entered my sights. At the gun's roar the buck jumped and bolted off through the hemlocks.

After calming down, I climbed from my stand and took up the trail. The long-tined eight-point went only 50 yards to a bed of leaves. His midday jaunt had been his downfall.

In a nocturnal buck's territory it's absolutely critical to cover up your scent and work the wind to your advantage. Both are basics of deer hunting, but I'm amazed at how many hunters overlook them. I place my tree stand at least 20 feet high, 20 to 60 yards (depending upon whether I'm bow or gun hunting) downwind of where I expect the buck to show, and cover my firearm or bow and my clothes with a good masking scent.

Because humans exhale more than 250 liters of air from their lungs per hour, I cover up my breath with chlorophyll gum or place a chunk of apple between my cheek and gum if apples are common to the area. Apples are great for killing bad breath. If you're not pre-pared to take these precautions, don't waste your time in a buck's sanctuary.

Stillhunting, though not as productive as stand hunting, can be an excellent option in a buck's bedroom on days when hunting pressure is light and deer are rarely forced to move. I always predetermine my route, sometimes months in advance, and slip through the bed-ding area at a snail's pace. If I cover more than 50 yards in an hour I know I'm going too fast.

Silent drives can also be productive in bedding areas. They can be accomplished with as few as two hunters in a number of ways. One is to have two hunters stillhunt single file through a bedding area 75 to 150 yards apart. Heading into or across the wind, the lead hunter may jump a deer, which will frequently circle back, giving the second hunter an opportunity for a shot.

Two other bedding area drives have either two to four hunters still-hunt toward each other or several hunters posted along known escape routes while several others stillhunt through the area. The key is to move slowly and quietly. In thick cover you'll never see more than pieces of a deer, usually one that's bedded. Also, whenever silent drives are conducted, hunter orange is a must to prevent accidents. Stillhunting is the ultimate test of woodsmanship when hunting a nocturnal buck and should only be tried in damp and windy conditions, when your stalking is least detectable.

To get a nocturnal buck's attention I often use a grunt tube and rattle antlers. Because of the different sounds deer make I prefer an adjustable grunt tube, one that can be blown with little effort yet be blown loudly without sounding like a duck call. An adjustable call enables you to make the grunt and mew of a doe as well as the grunt of a dominant buck, sounds that will often bring a rutting buck out of his bed.

Generally, I only use the grunt tube if I see or hear a deer first, and then I seldom blow on it more than five times. On occasion, however, I will use the grunt tube to initiate a response when I'm on the ground near a known sanctuary. I'll approach downwind and set up approximately 60 yards from where I think a buck might be. I'll grunt a few times and wait. I used this technique in a thick Saskatchewan swamp last November and had a nice eight-point grunt back to me. Now that's exciting!

Rattling in a nocturnal buck's bedroom can offer some memorable moments, too, but requires slightly more expertise than a grunt tube to avoid spooking the buck. The best time to rattle is 10 days before the peak of the rut, when scrapes are being actively worked. Bucks are searching for does at this time and because of their aggressive tendencies they'll often respond to rattling.

When whitetails are truly fighting they create a lot of noise. Five times in my life I've photographed two bucks in a real knock-down, drag-out fight. The noise they made was incredible! For this reason I rattle very aggressively. I like to tickle the tines together a few seconds before really getting into the loud stuff. Normally I rattle for about a minute, pause for about 30 seconds, rattle a minute, pause for 30 seconds, rattle for a minute, then put the antlers down and wait. I also offer a few low grunts with my tube while rattling to add more realism to the fight. If I'm on the ground I'll break brush and rake the ground. Unfortunately, however, ground rattling often allows the buck to spot you before you spot him. That's why I prefer to rattle from a tree when in a buck's sanctuary.

My 1992 New York shotgun season was a classic example of what hunting a nocturnal buck is all about. During July and August of that

HUNTING A BUCK'S BEDROOM

POST-SEASON

Using topo maps, aerial photos and on-foot scouting, locate active bedding areas in thick cover near food and water sources. Identify beds that host quality bucks, noting access and escape routes when deer are jumped.

EARLY SPRING

Locate old scrapes, rubs and active licking branches near the preferred bedding areas. Verify which are being tended by the largest deer by checking scrape tracks.

SUMMER

Choose stand placements and prepare core hunting areas by clearing multiple access trails to stand trees near bedding zones.

PRE-SEASON

Two weeks before the hunt, set up portable stands facing prevailing winds near bedding access trails. Scout from afar with optics, disturbing the areas as little as possible.

THE HUNT

Don't overhunt a bedding area, and stay on stand all day. Be especially mindful of wind direction and your scent—use quality masking scents on all equipment and apparel. With any luck, you'll have an old nocturnal buck in your crosshairs when hunting pressure forces him back to bed.

year three dandy bucks regularly fed in our hayfields. Though not pressured by me, they disappeared in September when small-game season began. Throughout bow season I hunted them hard but never saw them.

Because of the hunting pressure western New York receives, I hunted prime bedding areas from the opening day of shotgun season on. One location really appealed to me but, for fear of overhunting it, I

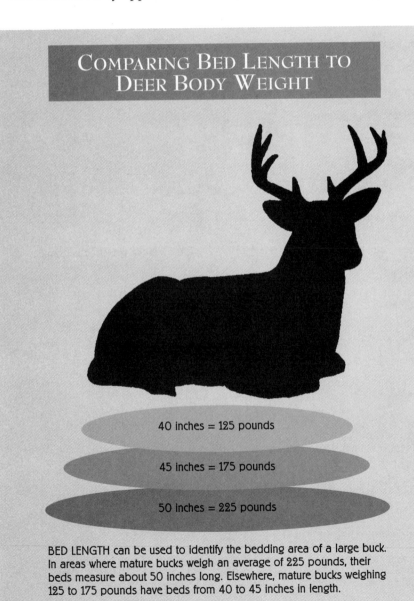

COMPARING BED LENGTH TO DEER BODY WEIGHT

40 inches = 125 pounds

45 inches = 175 pounds

50 inches = 225 pounds

BED LENGTH can be used to identify the bedding area of a large buck. In areas where mature bucks weigh an average of 225 pounds, their beds measure about 50 inches long. Elsewhere, mature bucks weighing 125 to 175 pounds have beds from 40 to 45 inches in length.

set up there only four of the first eight days. During those four days I passed up five yearling bucks and had many does within range. I decided to try it again Thanksgiving morning.

Turkey Day found me heading for the old hemlock tree anticipating great things, despite the weather. The day had dawned warm, damp and windless, not exactly the greatest hunting conditions . . . or so I thought. I slowly picked my way to the hemlock tree in the thickest part of the bedding area. I covered the 500 yards to the tree flawlessly, but in the pre-dawn darkness spooked a deer when I was halfway up the tree.

Not knowing what I had spooked, I readied myself for a long sit. About a half-hour after legal light I heard a lone grunt in the gully below. Due to the thick undergrowth I couldn't see a thing, but I knew that a buck was someplace out there. I brought my grunt tube to my lips and softly grunted twice. Within a minute I could see a wide-racked buck approaching stifflegged, his hair on end and ears pulled back. I brought my shotgun to my shoulder, put the crosshairs on his shoulder and fired. The big buck never knew what hit him.

Examining the buck I recognized him as one of the three I'd watched most of the summer. Though I had hunted him hard during bow season I never saw him until we crossed paths in the seemingly safe confines of his bedroom. He'd gone nocturnal, venturing from his sanctuary only under the cover of darkness. Fortunately, I was able to slip in and hunt him where he felt secure.

Nocturnal bucks are tough customers and demand all of the careful woodsmanship one can muster, but they can be hunted successfully if you remember the three keys: preparation, precaution and patience. One thing is certain, whether they live in Montana, Georgia or New York, nocturnals are the most challenging of all whitetails.

Outdoor Life, November 1993

ANTLERED GAME

Vanishing Whitetail

BY JIM ZUMBO

After chasing Coues deer in the Arizona desert, I now know why these animals are so tough to hunt.

I'm a great believer in glassing. I'd never go on a hunt without binoculars, and when I'm afield, they are almost in constant use. But this was insane.

In fact, I was sure that my guide, Dave Penrod, was asleep. He had been looking through his binoculars for a solid half hour and had hardly moved an inch the last 10 minutes. Lying prone on a big flat rock, elbows propping up his chin, his tripod-mounted binoculars were aimed at a mountain a half-mile away.

"Are you alive?" I whispered. "You can't make deer out of rocks, you know."

"Just another 10 minutes," Penrod said. "There's got to be some deer on that mountain. It looks too good."

I groaned a bit, got up and stretched muscles stiffened from being too long in an awkward position. Walking around a little rim, I approached George Taulman, my other companion. His eyes were also glued to binoculars. Like me, Taulman had never been on a Coues deer hunt before.

"It's not like looking for elk, is it George?" I said with a grin.

"Absolutely not," Taulman responded. "If elk were this tough to find, we'd never get any. These deer are invisible."

Taulman's assertion wasn't far from the truth. We were in Arizona after Coues deer, a whitetail subspecies known for its uncanny ability to blend in with its surroundings. Like apparitions, the few animals we'd spotted so far seemed to appear from out of nowhere.

First heralded by *Outdoor Life's* legendary former Shooting Editor Jack O'Connor, the Coues deer subspecies inhabits Arizona, New Mexico and Mexico. Similar in basic appearance to the whitetail, the Coues (pronounced either kooz or cows, depending on who you're talking to) sports antlers that are smaller than the typical mature whitetail buck. A 14 to 16-inch spread on a Coues is outstanding. If it sports 10 total points, you're looking at a whopper. The world-record Boone and Crockett Club buck scored 143 points and had an inside spread of only 15⅜. Body weight is also less than mature whitetails in most of its range. That may explain why I couldn't spot the darn things!

Getting here was hard enough. Although I had been interested in these little Southwestern deer for years, up to now I hadn't been lucky enough to draw a tag in the Arizona lottery. Using the services of Taulman's United States Outfitters (see box), I arranged for a hunt with outfitter Van Hale. That doesn't mean that taking or even seeing a Coues would be easy, however.

It took great effort to locate my first Coues deer. As the skies brightened on the first day of the hunt, Penrod and I took our perches atop a steep, rocky hillside to scan the country around us. The guide didn't budge for a full 35 minutes.

Seeing nothing, we moved on and repeated the glassing sessions with no luck, until Penrod finally spotted four deer a half-mile away. A small buck was standing still; three does were bedded. It took a few moments before I located the deer, and I was amazed that Penrod had seen them in the first place. The little grayish whitetails blended perfectly with the brush and rocks.

Getting to the deer was an ordeal, as tough as some of the elk and moose hunts I'd been on that fall. We gingerly descended a steep slope laced with large, loose rocks, crossed a small draw, and climbed up and over three small ridges. It was treacherous going all of the way, typical of good Coues country. Penrod and I slipped several times. By the time we got to where the deer had been, they had vanished. The rugged, noisy terrain had been our downfall.

We continued the same strategy for the next several days, spotting several animals, including some bucks. Because our hunting area had a history of yielding big bucks, we decided to wait for a better opportunity on a bigger animal.

My chance came on the last day—at least my watch indicated that it was daytime. A patchy, dense fog had moved in overnight and refused to burn off. We moved cautiously along the ridgetops, stopping to glass whenever the fog offered us a window. By midafternoon, visibility deteriorated, compounding the chore of spotting deer. The difficult-to-hunt country again proved to be our downfall.

As we approached a brushy ridgeline, a white-flagged lightning bolt erupted from the cover. The buck, a good one by Penrod's standards, allowed us to approach to within 10 yards before making a hasty exit. I was never able to draw a good bead on him.

I knew then that Jack O'Connor was right. Although I had barely scratched the surface of Coues deer hunting, chasing these little whitetails was the highlight of all of my fall hunts, which had included 11 states and three Canadian provinces. I'll be back for more.

Outdoor Life, July 1994

IF YOU CHOSE COUES

OBTAINING AN ARIZONA TAG REQUIRES A COMPUTER DRAW—ODDS AND SEASONS VARY BY UNIT. I CHOSE TO HUNT DURING THE WEEK OF CHRISTMAS TO COINCIDE WITH THE PEAK OF THE RUT. THE RELATIVE OPENNESS OF THE TERRAIN IN THE SOUTHWEST MEANS THAT YOU MUST BONE UP ON YOUR LONG-RANGE SHOOTING SKILLS. MOST HUNTERS PREFER .270, .280 OR .30-06 CALIBERS.

If you're confused about filling out big-game applications or have a habit of missing lottery deadlines, consider using the licensing service provided by United States Outfitters (800-845-9929). For a one-time fee, the service will prepare applications to hunt any species in practically all Western states. For example, if you want to apply for trophy muleys in limited-entry areas in several states, the service will send in your application automatically year after year until you draw.

Stalking the Tallgrass

BY MICHAEL PEARCE

Thanks to the federal CRP program, a new generation of world-class bucks are hiding in the flatlands.

The setup was as good as it gets. The stalk was as quiet as the gentle wind that fanned the sweat from my face. Rather than surrounded by a herd of watchful does, the mule deer buck was alone, bedded tight and looking in the opposite direction.

And this was not your typical make-a-nice-hat-rack deer. No, this was the kind of buck that fills your hopes and prayers during the long weeks and months before the fall seasons. Each time I caught a glimpse at the high and heavy rack, my eyes enlarged and my pulse went into overdrive. The rack extended well past the buck's over-sized ears. Beneath the antlers was an equally gargantuan body.

Mule deer of this caliber are very rare, indeed—the type of buck that would be tucked into the most rugged, primitive wilderness in the Rockies. Yet, there were no lofty mountain peaks, towering pines or jagged breaks with sage. The buck was living in flatland Kansas, where grain elevators constituted the highest topography. The buck was nestled in a broad field of waist-high prairie grasses typical of the fields enrolled in the U.S. Department of Agriculture's Conservation Reserve Program (CRP).

Like thousands of other sportsmen, I let out a shriek of joy, then began hoarding shotgun shells and training a new bird dog when the CRP portion of the 1985 Farm Bill passed in Washington. Simply put, the legislation was the USDA's way of checking soil erosion and crop surpluses across the country by paying farmers to take crop ground out of production. Farmers who signed up for the 10-year program were required to plant a cover crop of cane or maize the first year then drill native grass seed the next. Because it could never be grazed and only hayed under emergency conditions, these vast fields quickly added thousands of acres of habitat for wildlife. As hoped, the additional 36.5 million acres of native cover added to the heart of farm country have given us a glimpse of what the "good old days" of pheasant hunting must have been like some three decades ago.

Although not as anticipated or heralded, CRP fields have done even more for deer hunters. The lush grasses are yielding a new style of hunting that may forever be remembered as "the good old days." As it has for the long-tailed birds, the CRP fields have provided food and much-needed cover for wide-racked mule deer and whitetails.

Many big-game hunters saw, and still see, the vast tracts of grass as the ruination of their local deer hunting. Once easily found in the relatively few weedy draws, brushy creek bottoms and open pastures, the prairie deer seemed to disappear into the oceans of grass. Bucks that have literally been born and raised in the tallgrass cover have learned how to hide like never before. But some enterprising hunters have found ways to find the grass-loving bucks. Rich Pianalto, a friend and highly successful trophy mule deer guide and hunter, wasted little time showing me how to hunt the vast CRP fields near his Lakin, Kansas, home.

"The easiest way is to get on them early," he said as we planned our strategy before our first day of hunting. "I like to find a good buck that's coming back from feeding at first light and then watch him until he beds."

The first hint of dawn found us on a knoll using binoculars and a spotting scope to sweep the surrounding CRP fields. Even with the powerful optics it was no small task. Like many regions of agricultural America, the area held tens of thousands of acres of CRP land.

To make matters worse, much of the grass was chest-high. We were looking for antlers, ears, heads and necks rather than whole deer. In the land of legendary flatness, we used every elevation imaginable—

the tops of abandoned farm machinery, idle tractors and petroleum wells—to get a good look at the fields.

Finally, after spotting only does and small bucks and just before we surrendered the technique, Pianalto simply said, "There's what we're looking for." We closed the distance, set up a spotting scope and gave the buck a good look. He was a heavy-horned non-typical complete with honest wrist-thick mass, a variety of sticker points and a drop tine.

After the seeming eternity all sportsmen have experienced, the buck simply fell from sight. Rather than heading for the deer, Pianalto headed for a friend's farmyard for a soft drink and a chair. "It's best to give them a couple of hours to settle in," he explained. "He ought to be right in the middle of a nap when we come back."

When we returned I quickly learned the good news vs. bad news of stalking a buck bedded in CRP. On the positive side, the tallgrass makes for relatively quiet walking (especially when it's windy) and an unseen approach. But it also can make it tough to find bucks, even after you've watched them bed.

So it was that morning. We'd moved quickly into the general area but had been forced to slow to a snail's pace as we dissected the area step by step, looking for antler tips or the brown form of the bedded buck. We were just minutes away from closing in when an errant gust of wind took our scent to the big non-typical.

He rose 100 yards from where I stood and stared for several long seconds. Had I been carrying a centerfire rifle or a muzzleloader, the hunt would have been over. But because I was toting a bow, all I could do was watch as the buck bounded away.

As I later learned, catching a big buck on his early morning trip to his bedroom wasn't the only way to find a CRP buck. Weeks before the hunt, Pianalto had advised that I bring comfortable walking shoes. I'm glad I did.

If your eyes find no early morning bucks, it's time to switch the emphasis to your feet. Pianalto walks the fields with the methodical, back-and-forth pattern of a good pheasant hunter. Realizing that one field could take a half-day or more to cover, he scouts the area, looking for fresh tracks between the grass and potential feeding or watering areas.

But no matter how expansive the property is, he's learned the

STAYING LOW, Rich Pianalto begins a stalk on a mule deer buck bedded in CRP grass. At 30 yards from the deer, Pianalto comes to full draw, then elects not to shoot the modest-size buck. Good decision – a week later, still hunting CRP fields, Pianalto shot a non-typical muley that made the record book.

importance of a thorough search. "We're at a stage of the Conservation Reserve Program now where some of these really big bucks have been born and raised in this grass," Pianalto said. "They've learned to hold tight. They'll let you walk right past them."

One afternoon, we experienced such a close encounter after pulling Pianalto's pickup to the edge of a 160-acre CRP field. Looking to my left, not 25 yards away, I spotted a gray face and a huge set of antlers mixed in with the tawny grasses. Had we kept driving, the buck no doubt would have held his ground.

But when Pianalto braked his rig, the big muley rose and trotted off. What I'd first perceived as a blunder turned into a good lesson. Rather than flee the county, the big bruiser trotted another 300 yards and disappeared.

"What happened?" I asked.

"He bedded down again," said Pianalto. "Unless you really scare them, they usually won't go far. They feel pretty safe in the CRP." Pianalto then explained the benefit of hunting in pairs, often leaving one hunter at a vantage point to watch deer that can pull some surprising moves.

Late one afternoon we jumped a dandy buck and watched him trot off toward the middle of a field. With darkness threatening, we only waited 30 minutes before we began our stalk. To our surprise, we were almost run over by the buck just 100 yards from where we'd jumped him! It was obvious he was circling around to bed in the same area again.

Although the true trophy bucks seldom rise on their own from daytime beds, smart hunters have learned to let smaller deer lead them to trophies. During the rut, for instance, it is wise to stalk what appears to be an unchaperoned cluster of does. Chances are good Mr. Big is lying in the grass nearby.

Early in the fall, when the dominant bucks are still tolerating their smaller-horned grandchildren and great-grandchildren, following a raghorn buck could lead to a trophy. We tried this tactic one after-noon last fall. A 3x3 rose from the edge of a CRP field in front of us, but he seemed in no hurry as he dropped into a dry creek bed. Figuring that he might have company nearby, Pianalto and I sneaked to the lip of the eroded bank, peeked over, and saw the smallish buck standing with a huge buck with a great set of antlers. As luck would have it, the 3x3 moved on but the larger-racked buck only nestled further down into the grass.

As described earlier, it was a perfect setup. The wind stayed in my face as I stalked quietly, using a break in the terrain to shield my approach. In the tallgrass, getting a clear shot can be tougher than getting in range because the cover can obscure much of a buck's body.

In the past, Pianalto has used a bleat call to get a big buck to rise from its bed. But it wasn't needed on my stalk. When I was 30 yards away, the big buck obligingly stood and looked in the direction of the 3x3. In less time than it takes to tell, my arrow found its mark.

The buck was truly the kind most of us hope for. The massive beams spread 29 inches and carried some long, widely spread forks. Even with a broken tine, the buck would easily make the Pope and Young Club bowhunting record book. Just as impressive as the headgear was the buck's massive body. With a field-dressed weight right at 300 pounds, Pianalto and I needed every bit of adrenaline we had to drag the buck out of the field.

Trophy bucks are far from a fluke in CRP. That day alone we'd seen three or four other "book" bucks in the big patches of grass. A week later, while I was working on this text, Pianalto called on his mobile phone to tell me he'd just arrowed a 28-inch-racked non-typical that would also make the Pope and Young Club record book. The follow-ing day he called again, this time with news of a phenomenal CRP bow-killed mule deer that green-scored nearly 200 Pope and Young points. The buck was later officially scored at 202⅝ points, demolish-ing the existing Kansas record (also a CRP buck), and ranking as the second largest bow-killed mule deer ever recorded.

Big mule deer from big grass fields come not only from Kansas. "It's fabulous!" said Jamie Byrne, a highly respected guide from Mill Iron, Montana. "We've totally changed our style of hunting and now base it on the CRP. The deer have really moved out there and stayed. We're very, very successful in the CRP." Similar glowing reports are also coming from the Dakotas, Colorado, Texas and Nebraska, and large tracts of CRP are scattered throughout the West and Midwest.

And CRP is not only successful for muleys—whitetails are also thriving.

"There's no doubt the [Conservation Reserve] program has had a big effect on the whitetails where I hunt in northern Missouri and other Midwestern states," said Toby Bridges, well-kown muzzleloading expert and trophy deer hunter. "The deer really use [CRP] in areas that were previously planted with heavy agriculture mixed with small plots of standing timber. The CRP grass gives them a good edge habitat. As long as they aren't pressured too hard, they'll really, really use it." Bridges said that Midwestern hunters are also beginning to utilize the grassy fields.

"Some whitetail hunters are using spot-and-stalk and some are using drives effectively," he said. "Others, especially bowhunters who get to hunt undisturbed whitetails, are doing well setting up between food sources and CRP bedding areas. Smart hunters are adapting almost as fast as the whitetails have."

Even as America becomes increasingly urbanized, CRP has arrived as an outlet valve for deer and deer hunters. The success of this conservation program is changing the face of deer hunting and adding an enormous amount of land with trophy buck potential.

Next time you dream about that buck of a lifetime, your focus may change from a scene of Rocky Mountain rimrock or Midwestern swamp timber to a grassy flat plain where the tips of massive antlers rise barely into view. The proof has already been shown, and there are 36 million acres to choose from. (Editor's note: Turn the page and read how two hunters scored big—real big—in CRP.)

Outdoor Life, August 1993

New Records from CRP

TWO BOWHUNTERS FROM TINY SCOTT CITY, KANSAS, MAY HAVE KICKED OFF A REVOLUTION IN HUNTING RECORD-CLASS MULE DEER. IN A SPAN OF LESS THAN THREE WEEKS, THEY MORE THAN PROVED THAT THE LUSH GRASSLANDS OF THE CONSERVATION RESERVE PROGRAM CAN PRODUCE THE LARGEST TROPHY MULE DEER IN THE WORLD.

It all began when Stacy Hoeme, a veteran trophy bowhunter, was on a combination crop-checking/deer-hunting excursion last October. He spotted a herd of mule deer and stalked to within 30 yards. In the herd were a high-scoring typical, a fine non-typical and a smaller buck. He passed up an easy shot on the typical just before the herd spooked.

Knowing the land and the habits of its deer, Hoeme followed the herd and found them bedded in a field of CRP grass. After a diligent stalk, and encounters with an assortment of cactus and burrs, the bowhunter took a 30-yard shot at the bedded non-typical. The 12x11-point muley's official net score of 226²/₈ made it the best of its kind taken in America in 1992 and the second largest

non-typical mule deer ever taken in Kansas by a bowhunter.

As impressive as the deer was, Hoeme's deer was overshadowed by bowhunter Carl Ghan Jr.'s achievement on October 25, 1992. Ghan was glassing a broad expanse of CRP field in Gove County, Kansas, when he spotted a mixed herd of muley does and bucks. One of the bucks looked particularly large, so he began a stalk after the deer had bedded.

As Ghan neared the area where the deer had been bedded, none were in sight. The grass was so dense and high that he feared the herd had spooked and left unseen. When he stood to survey the situation he saw the big typical bedded just a few feet away. Ghan wasted no time in shooting the mule deer that carried an elk-size rack.

With an official score of 202⁶/₈, Ghan's 7x6-point buck shattered the existing state records for both gun and bow, and the deer was less than one-half inch short of tying the existing Pope and Young Club world record. The buck now stands as No. 2, and provides a tremendous vote of confidence for the conservation success of the CRP program.

In the dense tall grasses the future for trophy mule deer and whitetails is very bright indeed.

So You Want to Hunt the New Muleys

BY JIM ZUMBO

*Mule deer have evolved
at genetic warp speed,
so your hunting tactics
must also change.*

"Mule deer are dumb," the man said. "Stupid. They live in open country and aren't afraid of hunters. There's no challenge to hunting them."

It turns out this pontificating gentleman based his low opinion of mule deer on one western hunting trip made back in the mid-60s when muleys were notoriously unwary. Truth be told, in those days I held much the same opinion. When I moved from the East Coast to the West in 1960 I found big buck muleys plentiful—and in comparison with whitetails, not terribly intelligent.

While I can't say I was surprised by the man's attitude, I was amazed when he refused to acknowledge that mule deer hunting has changed greatly over the past few decades. Unfortunately, he's not alone. Plenty of people who haven't recently hunted muleys continue to believe that the big-racked bucks of the West are pushovers.

Nothing could be further from the truth. Nowadays the vast majority of hunters return from a mule deer trip with either no deer or only small bucks. Consider this sobering statistic: Across the West, the average hunter-success rate for muley bucks is only 30 percent—7 out of 10 hunters come back emptyhanded. The success rate for a buck with antlers 26 inches wide is 5 to 10 percent in most states.

And the 30-inch buck—the one everyone dreams about? The odds on finding him are off the board.

Unsuccessful hunters make two basic mistakes: They hunt the wrong country, and they don't hunt correctly. Logic dictates that in order to take a good muley you must hunt where it lives and know how to find it. Merely hunting a place known to harbor deer no longer will get the job done.

One of the toughest chores for the newcomer to mule deer is to evaluate bucks. Because mule deer typically have higher and wider racks than whitetails, it's easy for the inexperienced hunter or—sometimes worse—a longtime whitetail hunter to be fooled into thinking he is staring at a trophy animal. Even a so-so muley looks impressive to a first-timer. Many hunters take the first buck they see and lament their rashness later.

I remember an incident that occurred a dozen years ago when I guided a pal from the East on a Colorado mule deer hunt. He was an official measurer for the Boone and Crockett Club and had scored many big muleys, but had never set foot in the West until our hunt. When a three-by-three buck bounced out of heavy cover, my friend opted to pass, hoping for a four-pointer. Our agreement was that I'd shoot only if he got a deer first or passed up a shot. My back was acting up at the time and I was more interested in meat than horns, so I took the buck. It was a dandy, with a 27-inch spread and plenty of mass. My companion was clearly impressed with the three-pointer.

The next day he indeed shot a four by four but with a spread of only 21 inches. "I didn't know four-point mules could be so small," he said. It was the first four-pointer he'd seen on the trip, and he reacted too quickly. I felt a bit guilty because I had sent the deer his way without advising him about the buck's relatively small headset. And wouldn't you know it? We saw several four-pointers after that, each of them much bigger than his.

Option Play

These days, hunters would love the option of picking and choosing bucks. Unfortunately, that's rarely the case, even in country that previously offered prime hunting for big bucks.

The decline in numbers, as well as the quality of muley, is attributable to several factors. Human encroachment on habitat, diseases, parasites, predators, hunting pressure, drought, and severe winter weather are the major culprits—with the latter two sharing most of the blame. Most experts believe that these weather cycles will continue to occur, and that the banner years of the 1950s and '60s are gone forever.

A new breed of mule deer has evolved at genetic warp speed. It has taken these deer only three decades to adjust from passive, prepressure dolts to modern-day geniuses of evasion. They behave far differently than their recent ancestors. Consequently, the hunter must radically modify his approach to mule deer hunting, beginning with the planning process and not ending until his finger squeezes the trigger. He who doesn't will be among the 70 out of 100 hunters who won't get their bucks this autumn.

Borderline Politics

While the muley has become more wily, man has also had a hand in the species' changed status. In the West, all states are not created equal. You can count on mule deer hunting changing dramatically when you cross a border, depending on the state's wildlife politics, hunting pressure, and habitat.

It's no great secret that your best chance at quality animals is in country where hunting pressure is limited or restricted. This translates to either private land, public land where there is a quota of permits, or public land that, for reasons I'll explain, doesn't attract very many hunters.

If you really want a challenge, try finding a big buck muley in a national forest where deer tags are unlimited during the general season. Disneyland has smaller crowds.

Why do so many people jam into public areas? Primarily because they don't know private landowners, can't afford to hire an outfitter, or haven't drawn a tag in a limited-entry area and haven't taken the time in the off-season to prepare.

Here's another surprise awaiting you. Western hospitality is usually wonderful, but not when it comes to getting permission to hunt someone's private property. In prime mule deer country you're apt to see as many posted signs as you would in the suburbs of Pittsburgh. Leasing has become a big deal in the West. Many ranchers now charge fees to hunt, and some of those fees are amazingly high in good hunting country.

My favorite strategy to beat the crowds is to apply for quality tags in units having quotas. If I'm lucky enough to draw, the potential of meeting up with a good buck is excellent, and the solitude offered by fewer hunters is a definite bonus. Every state offers limited-entry areas requiring a lottery draw for a tag.

Here again planning and homework will help you find those places. Don't be afraid to call wildlife agencies and ask for information. Most government wildlife biologists welcome the opportunity to chat with hunters. But let's say you have no choice but to hunt public land with unlimited tags. There is still a chance for you to be among the elite 30 percent of successful hunters, but you must be determined to hunt smart and different.

The best way not to get a buck is to cruise the roads along with all those other hunters, hoping you spot a deer. Instead, get off your tail, out of the vehicle and into places other hunters ignore. Stay off trails, old roads, and other convenient human paths. Work your way into brush, thickets, blowdowns, and places with heavy cover.

While you're at it, be aware that the new breed of muley is far less apt to spook from cover as he might have 20 years ago. The modern mule buck is likely to hide, just like the whitetail you hunt at home.

It goes without saying that the older the buck, the tougher he'll be to find. I've outsmarted deer in public areas by using human traffic to push deer to me. At other times I've done just the opposite. Wary deer seek places where they're least disturbed; many times those are sparse areas that border prime "deer country." Big bucks are known to leave their regular haunts and journey to barren-looking places that most hunters pass by.

We humans tend to focus our efforts in places that "look" good. I've spent a good share of my time successfully hunting muleys in low benchlands, arid pinyon-juniper forests, dusty sagebrush expanses, and greasewood deserts. Meanwhile, the other hunters drove madly past those spots to seek deer in the lush higher elevations. Of my top five muley buck takes, one came from a limited-entry area, one from private land, and three from marginal, untraditional areas on public land.

Here's another tip: Most general rifle hunts occur in early to mid-October. This is a tough time to hunt because deer are scattered throughout their vast home range. Astute hunters look for big bucks late in the fall on their much smaller winter range.

By hunting from mid- to late November in states or areas that offer late-season hunts, and getting a break from Mother Nature in the form of substantial snowfall, you'll find deer far more accessible as well as vulnerable. Heavy snows drive deer from the higher elevations down to lowland areas. The trick is, of course, to have fresh snow when you are in the field. Obviously you can't count on it, but chances are far greater to have deep snow late in the season than earlier.

Combine that migrating pattern out of the snow with the rut season and you have a scenario that shouts big bucks. The muley rut goes strong from mid-November into December, causing the biggest bucks to lose most of their natural caution. For these brief few weeks, their primary objective in life is to find and breed as many does as possible. Unlike whitetails, which can be hunted over scrapes and rubs and can be called and rattled in, muleys offer few similar opportunities. They don't make scrapes, their rubs have no significant purpose for hunting strategies, they don't respond well to calls, and I've found they aren't much interested in rattling antlers. What this usually means to the hunter is a rugged quest in deep snow, perhaps following fresh tracks, perhaps making a stalk on a previously spotted deer, and most definitely employing binoculars. Remember that your odds get better in direct proportion to the time you spend afoot, climbing and descending mountains, sneaking through timber, and relentlessly looking for your prize, which may be just over the next ridge.

The bottom line in modern mule deer hunting is this: Do not think that muleys are easy customers. Prepare yourself to be as physically tough as you can, do your homework when planning a trip, and hunt smart. There are still plenty of big bucks out there, but the modern muley has an IQ that requires you to smarten up.

Outdoor Life, September 1995

Battling Blacktails

BY JIM ZUMBO

*What makes the mule
deer's cousin the
toughest trophy of all?
Everything!*

Blacktail deer suffer from a popularity problem—outside their range,
no one knows much about them.
The deer are inhabitants of the West Coast,
from central California north through
Oregon, Washington and British Columbia.

Within much of that vast north-south finger of land, blacktails dwell
in the most incredibly thick cover you can imagine. A good share of
this habitat is rain-forest country, where you will do well to be able to
walk on the floor of the planet for more than a few minutes at a time.
Mostly, you'll be crawling on downed logs that are greasy with moss
and soaked from constant rains. When you're fortunate enough to be
on the ground for more than five yards at a stretch, you'll be fighting
Devil's Club, a horrid plant that grows spines that reach out and grab
you regardless of how careful you are. Brambles and briers from a
dozen other plants await, along with jungles of wet ferns and vines
and zillions of baseball-bat-thick trees that form impenetrable walls.

Blacktail deer do live in this jungle, however, and some hunters do
hunt them in it. Having worked in such conditions, in Oregon as a
young forester more than 30 years ago (my partner and I had to use
headlamps in the daytime to see each other in the underbrush five
yards apart), and having hunted blacktails a number of times, I

salute those folks who really get into the jungles and hunt. There aren't many of them; most hunters who experience these nightmarish tangles once or twice don't want any more. They hunt clear-cuts by walking and driving along logging roads. Or they abandon blacktail country altogether, and either hunt muleys in the eastern, more open, parts of their states or, as is the case with Californians, they head for Colorado and other states where the hunting is more hospitable.

Ray Croswell is a good example of a dedicated blacktail hunter. A Washington native, he takes some dandy bucks each year. He hunts public land, and he seldom sees another hunter.

Most of Croswell's success is due to his ability to find deer, which in turn is almost solely a search for numerous rubs. He drives logging roads until he finds several rubbed trees and then parks his vehicle and heads off into the bush, staying on trails when possible. Most of his prime hunting is in mid to late November, when blacktails are in the rut. He continues his search for more rubs, and when he locates them he settles in and stillhunts those spots. He moves away from trails when necessary and chooses areas on fairly open slopes wherever possible, hoping to catch feeding deer early in the morning.

I've hunted with Croswell many times, and I'm amazed at his ability and willingness to attack this inhospitable country. He's the kind of guy who leaves the road before daylight, is immediately swallowed up in the woods and reappears after dark from an entirely different direction.

If you try this and are a bit unsettled at being in thick forests with no landmarks, use a good map and compass. Don't rely on following trails because situations may present themselves where you'll have to leave a trail to follow a wounded deer or simply to investigate other parts of your hunting country where good trails don't exist.

Should you wish to eliminate hunting in heavy brush altogether, walk old logging roads behind locked gates. Many national forests allow only foot or horseback travel on roads that lead to logged areas. I know one spot where a three-mile walk down a logging road will get me away from most other hunters and into plenty of deer in a clear-cut. When you do this, leave your vehicle well before dawn in order to be in your hunting area by first light.

The California Connection

Looking for blacktails in the rain forest and adjacent clear-cuts was the only way I knew how to hunt these deer. But I was aware that

BEST COUNTIES FOR BLACKTAILS

ACCORDING TO THE SECOND EDITION OF THE BOONE AND CROCKETT CLUB'S *RECORDS OF THE NORTH AMERICAN ELK AND MULE DEER,* THE TOP BLACKTAIL TROPHIES COME FROM THE FOLLOWING COUNTIES IN CALIFORNIA, OREGON AND WASHINGTON. THIS EDITION HAS A MINIMUM SCORE OF 120, WHILE THE ALL-TIME BOOK HAS A MINIMUM OF 130.

Washington counties:
Lewis and Pierce

Oregon counties:
Clackamas, Linn and Marion

Josephine and Jackson

California counties:
Trinity, Humboldt and Siskiyou

Mendocino

■ RANGE OF BLACKTAIL DEER

California (345 entries): Top counties (in order of most entries)—Trinity, Mendocino, Humboldt and Siskiyou. Of the top-10 all-time-record California bucks, Siskiyou County had four while Trinity County had three.

Oregon (250 entries): Top counties (in order of most entries)—Jackson, Clackamas, Linn, Marion and Josephine. Of the top-10 all-time-record Oregon bucks, Jackson had three and Marion County had two.

Washington (154 entries): Top counties (in order of most entries)—Lewis and Pierce. Of the top-10 bucks, Lewis had four entries.

BINOCULARS are a must for finding long-distance blacktails in clear-cuts and other open areas.

they're hunted in a very different landscape in parts of California. For years, I'd talked to pals who pursue the deer in enormous open stretches, where vast fields of wild oats blanket steep hills and forests of oak trees and other hardwood species grow in the draws and valley bottoms. This, I thought, had to be blacktail heaven, where a person actually saw the sun, wasn't constantly soaked by rain and didn't have to carry an oversized first-aid kit to treat the wounds from the hazards of the rain forest.

I finally got around to trying out that country last summer, when I was invited by Nick Tacito, president of the Golden Ram Club in Northern California (650-692-6670). The club, which has about 550 members, allows hunting on leased private lands. Though plenty of blacktails inhabit California's national forests, the best hunting is on private property, which is no different than in most other parts of the country. Since I'd already hunted California's public land in years past, I was curious about what the private property had to offer.

I was accompanied by Ed Rice, who runs several sportsmen's shows in the West. We joined Nick and other club members on one of their leased ranches. It was a September hunt, and the temperature was approaching 100 degrees. That's not unusual for California blacktail trips, since many seasons open in August.

Spot and Stalk

Hunting those deer was nothing like chasing their brethren in the coastal rain forests. This was extremely steep country, where long-distance walking in uneven terrain was the norm. Unlike coastal hunting—where you cover very little ground in a day with marginal visibility—here we hiked in the blazing sun, using binoculars to spot deer at long distances early in the morning and late in the afternoon.

As it turned out, I managed to tag a modest three-point buck. He was grazing in a draw just after daybreak, and I put him down with a 150-yard shot from my .270. My attitude on blacktails is to take the first legal buck that shows up. Though I might have waited for a bigger buck on this property, Nick was concerned that the heat might put a damper on deer movement. He was right, since no bigger bucks were spotted the next few days, although some fine blacktails traditionally come from the ranch we hunted.

I'm not sure I'll hunt with Nick again. His lovely wife sent home-cooked meals to camp, and I had to begin a serious diet when the hunt was over, despite all the strenuous hiking. Golden Ram members normally bring their own campers and follow ranch rules for each property. I was impressed with this operation, which seems to be a good opportunity for California hunters.

Compared to their bigger mule deer cousins, West Coast blacktails may not have the body size or large antlers, but they make up for it in the terrain they inhabit and their behavior. These deer are masters at hiding and sneaking, and if I didn't know any better, I'd swear a whitetail or two infused a couple genes somewhere along the line. More than once I figured blacktails were nothing more than white-tails in disguise.

Outdoor Life, November 1997

Elk on Your Own

BY RON SPOMER

*You don't need to spend a
ton of money and hire a
guide to have a successful
elk hunt. All you need is
to plan and work hard.*

They say that the whitetail is the
most popular big-game animal on
this continent, but I'll bet that more
hunters dream about and drool over bull
elk than buck deer.

You can generally see a whitetail a mile from the house, but an elk—
now there's a wild animal. Six hundred pounds of raw wilderness
roaring in the mountains. Three, four, five feet of antler gleaming
in the sun, tearing at the earth, ripping, gouging and snapping
three-inch trees. The royal pinnacle of deer evolution in the New
World. Elk.

Isn't it exciting to know that you alone—or you and a partner—can
tag your bull without selling your firstborn child to finance a full-
blown, guided, wrangled, horse-and-tent mountain hunt? Isn't it
comforting to know that you don't have to pay a trespass fee or ask
for hunting permission? Just do your homework, practice a few simple techniques, shape up, pack your camping gear and go get 'em.

Really. A successful elk hunt can be just that easy.

Of course, your favorite hunting partner could ruin the hunt. Then
again, he could improve it. Depends on how intelligently you plan

and work together—or apart. And that's the key to this whole one- or two-man elk hunting business—working and planning intelligently.

Like many sportsmen east of the Rockies, I thought that a six-point elk was an expensive, unattainable goal. How was I ever going to learn where and how to hunt them without professional guidance? I went on one ill-prepared trip to Montana in 1976 just to prove myself right, then sat back to wring my hands and wonder. In 1986, however, I tried it again, first with two partners as green as I in an area we'd never seen before, then all alone two weeks later. I drove home with a 6x7 bull. The amazing thing was that I could have shot four more.

Why the quick success on just my second try? Because since 1976, I'd really been doing a bit more than wringing my hands; I'd been studying elk. By 1985, I knew as much about elk as they did. I knew where they ate, where they bedded, where they ran and what they said.

I also knew how to hunt them, thanks to magazine articles, books and long conversations with veteran elk hunters. Game department officials had willingly told me where branch-antlered bulls concentrated. Elk in parks and zoos had tuned me in to their grunts, bugles, barks and whines, and a calling seminar at a local bowhunting shop had taught me how to imitate those sounds. I did my homework, and it paid off, just as it can for anyone.

A good place to start is right where you are—reading. Magazine articles are always good, as are books about elk hunting. Buy them from a club or bookstore or borrow from a library, but don't read just for entertainment. Study. Take notes. Record what each author recommends. Not all will agree, for there are many ways to hunt elk. One man's most successful technique may be another's standing joke. What works in Arizona may fail miserably in Alberta. Your job is to glean the tactics that work in the area and during the season you plan to hunt.

Selecting that area and season will entail some effort. You'll need to write a few letters or make a few phone calls. Experienced elk hunters are always worth contacting. But be certain that they know what they're talking about. You won't get much help from Henry Slovenly, who's been wearing out tires on Colorado logging roads for a decade and finally stumbled across a ragged four-pointer last year. You need to talk to real hunters, men and women who have climbed the mountains, followed the tracks, located the wallows, heard the bugles and seen the quarry again and again. They'll know the habits of elk and where and when to find them.

Do-it-yourself hunters usually are most successful in the early seasons because the weather is milder. Outfitters and some locals may be able to leave a snowed-in camp or vehicle until the spring thaw, but most sportsmen need their rigs to drive back home. If possible, plan a mid-September to early October hunt, when bugling bulls are easy to locate. After mid-October, they can be disgustingly elusive until heavy snows drive them to lower elevations.

Generally, you can expect the most and biggest bulls where hunting pressure is lowest. On public land, this means inaccessible terrain or a carefully regulated harvest, and here the game departments can help out. They keep records of such things as harvest, winter populations, bull/cow ratios, and so on. Ask the persons in the state where you plan to hunt which units during the past five years have provided the most or largest branch-antlered bulls per hunter, and which have the highest bulls-per-cow ratio.

Obviously, your odds of finding a bull should be higher in a hunting unit with 30 bulls per 100 cows than one with 10 bulls per 100 cows, all other things being equal. It pays to ask the game department why high bull/cow ratios came to be. If it's because of restricted harvest or light hunting pressure, make room in the freezer. If the best-populated units are too steep or thickly forested to hunt, however, you're better off working a more reasonable terrain with slightly fewer bulls.

Unless you're an Ironman triathlete or have a string of pack animals, you won't want to hunt units 20 miles from a road. Yes, these usually see slightly less hunting pressure than do roadside units, but they're tough to reach, and the professional guides and outfitters who elect to hunt them can harvest mature bulls more effectively than average hunters often do in more accessible areas. The drainage in which I called five bulls within bow range last year lies just two miles from a major Forest Service road.

Don't take this distance consideration lightly. It could make or break your solo or duet hunt. Remember, not only do you have to carry a light camp into a distant hunting unit, but you also have to carry an elk out. Believe me, elk carcasses don't come in lightweight backpacker models. The trick, then, is to identify a hunting unit with a combination of good road access, high bull/cow ratio, history of yielding branched bulls, and lots of ridges or isolated valleys.

Why the ridges and valleys? Because they act as barriers to hunters and security for elk. The big deer like to put a solid ridge or two between themselves and man, and man likes to put no ridges between himself and his vehicle. If you can find a series of ridges within a few miles of a road, you should be able to find elk within a reasonable day's hike.

While you're researching where to hunt, train your body to be able to hunt. Mountains demand a lot of leg, a lot of lung and a lot of stamina. Start early to develop those with a regimen of running, biking or swimming and weight lifting. Squeeze in as much backpacking and steep-grade climbing as you can. Push yourself. Get tough, then get tougher. Your quarry will be.

Long before your hunt, assemble your home-away-from-home. Any tent or camper is suitable as long as it provides enough room to cook, eat, sleep and dry gear. The leakiest tent will stay dry if you erect it under a waterproof tarp. Take lots of tarps. Make sure that your lanterns and stoves work, and make sure that you have all the pots, pans, saws, axes, shovels, ropes, and other gear you'll need. In short, prepare yourself for getting into and out of high, rugged country where it may snow or rain for a week, and have what you need to live there for two weeks in case you can't get out.

The same advice applies to backpack camps. You can carry only a minimum, so be certain that everything functions perfectly. And pack an extra, light rain fly under which you can store gear and cook if it rains.

Prospecting hunters who live near their elk can benefit from advanced scouting and preliminary camp construction. Backpack into your hunting area to familiarize yourself with the terrain. Note the brushy and grassy feeding areas, the dense loafing cover and the trails.

Now, will you go it alone or take a partner? Doubling up is great for sharing expenses and workload—an elk comes out of the woods twice as fast with two guys packing—but solo has its benefits, too. For one thing, a lone hunter sets his own pace, hunting as hard or easy as he wants. He also hones his woodsmanship, for there is no one else on whom to lean. The solo hunter worries only about himself and his quarry. There's no need to wonder whether Jim made it over the ridge yet, whether he's moving in on that bugling bull or whether you should, whether he's hurt out in the dark or merely late getting back to camp. Alone, you hunt more efficiently because you concentrate better and make less of a disturbance.

Last fall, I had a big six-point bull thrashing a pine 100 yards in front of me, and there was more than enough cover to take me within 25 yards of him. But my partner had also heard the ruckus, and he tried slipping in from an open slope on the other side. When I was 50 yards away and closing, the bull saw Neil and thundered out of there.

Accidents like that don't have to happen. Partners should anticipate conflicts ahead of time, discuss them and plan to avoid them. One option is to share camp but hunt in different directions. Another is to coordinate efforts and hunt side by side, playing off one another to dupe elk.

One of the most successful buddy systems entails splitting up to locate elk, then cooperating to hunt them. During the bugle season, one man sets up for a shot while the other calls behind him. Approaching bulls key on the caller, and the shooter generally aims and shoots unnoticed from close range. We used this technique last year to put Neil within spitting range of a young four-pointer.

Three of us hadn't seen an elk in five days of rainy, snowy hunting, but on the sixth day I found myself in the middle of a talkative herd of bulls. I threw an arrow over a five-pointer walking uphill directly toward me at 23 yards, passed up a standing spike at 30 yards, and spooked two more branched bulls at close range before strategically retreating to camp for reinforcements, Bill and Neil—who didn't believe me.

"I'm not kidding," I argued. "They're all over that mountainside. I'm telling you, I missed a nice five-pointer at 25 yards. Look, one of my arrows is missing. Would a cheapskate like me waste an arrow on anything but an elk?"

We made the four miles back to the elk by 3:30. I got an answer on my first bugle.

"There they are. See? You guys spread out about 50 yards and set up about 20 yards ahead of me."

It happened fast. I bugled, he bugled. I grunted. I mewed like a cow. Antlers bobbed over the brush. Neil hunkered behind a tree trunk. The four-pointer stepped clear, looking for me. He walked a half-circle around Neil, and then I stopped him with a mew call—16 steps from Neil, the former tournament shooter who has asked me not to tell how he missed that broadside shot.

Although elk bugling has been an effective tactic for decades, the new natural-sounding calls have made it deadlier than ever. If you've never heard a diaphragm or grunt-tube call, buy an elk-calling instruction tape and listen up. You can't distinguish a good caller from a real elk, and neither can the elk.

Despite what you may have heard, raging, passionate, frustrated bulls do not always charge a challenger. In fact, young bulls will avoid what sounds to them like older, stronger bulls, and the herd masters will often, if not usually, run off with their harems rather than risk losing them to a rival.

To lure the satellite bulls, try to sound just a tad smaller so they'll think they can take out their frustrations on you. It doesn't hurt to throw in a few cow mews. Those always calm spooky bulls and usually lure them closer.

Herd bulls may require aggressive calling and physical pushing. If you start a conversation with a strong bull that comes no closer or moves away, get after him, squealing and raging and beating the brush, taunting him and getting so close that he has to turn on you to protect his interests.

After our botched bowhunt, I returned to the area for the opening of rifle season and heard three bugling bulls within two miles of the road. After talking with them for a half-hour, I determined that they weren't coming any closer, so I tried silently, slowly sneaking in. The gap widened as they continued down the mountain. I finally threw caution to the winds and crashed through the timber after them, eventually bumping into a herd of cows that threatened to spook the whole mountain clean.

Thank heavens for the cow mew call. With four of the old girls staring me cold, I squeaked a few reassuring mews over the diaphragm caller in my mouth, and they bought it. Must have mistaken me for one ugly lost cousin. As soon as they fed out of sight, I trotted toward the bull that was still roaring up ahead. I screamed back. That did it. Now I was too close, and he turned to take a stand, raking the timber with his antlers, honing them before running me through. I checked my chamber for that reassuring flash of brass, then grunted five times and mewed like a misbehaving cow. Bingo! One big bull stepped into the open . . . .

I just wish that there would've been someone to help me carry him out.

When elk are silent, two men can drive them if one posts along an escape trail while the other circles and attempts a stalk. Should the stalker fail, he'll often push the elk toward his waiting partner. One man can also play "lookout," watching a distant bull as his partner stalks and guiding him as necessary with hand signals.

Elk aren't homebodies the way whitetails are, but they do use trails consistently between feeding and loafing cover if left undisturbed for several days. A stint of stand hunting is welcome after several days of climbing mountains.

When one or two hunters kill an elk, the real work begins. This is the worst part of a horseless hunt. That behemoth must be butchered, cooled and transported to a road, and you're the only jackass likely to volunteer. Don't balk. It's not as difficult as it first seems.

Gut the carcass and bone it immediately, muscle group by muscle group. You must get the meat away from the bones, where body heat remains long enough to induce spoilage. Place these easily handled hunks of meat in the shade on clean grass, leaves, or muslin cloth or plastic brought along for this purpose. Keep the hunks separate overnight or until cooled through. Then, pile as many as you can carry into garbage bags or muslin sacks placed inside a backpack, and walk out. It should take you four or five trips alone, two or three with a partner. Don't forget the rack.

At camp, place the meat into a cooler and surround it with ice; it will keep for several days to a week. Prop those magnificent antlers against a tree, lean back and relax. You can stop drooling and dreaming now. Your planning and hard work have paid off.

Who said that elk were so tough and expensive?

Outdoor Life, May 1987

Bull of the Century

BY MERWIN MARTIN AS TOLD TO JIM ZUMBO

It took me 35 years to set my sights on a trophy elk, but when I finally did, the bull turned out to be Wyoming's biggest in more than a century.

It was just breaking day when I spotted eight bull elk feeding in a drainage that protected them from fierce early morning winds. There was no doubt in my mind that one of the bulls was the biggest I'd ever seen in a lifetime of hunting.

I was after mule deer on the last day of the season, but I forgot about muleys and immediately set up my spotting scope. The general elk season was closed, but I'd drawn a late season tag for this particular area, and the hunt would start in a week.

"Is that bull as big as I think he is?" I said to my pal Harold Liner as I focused the spotting scope. A few moments later, with the bull in the scope, I was astounded. I could hardly believe my eyes. When Harold looked at the bull, he had the same reaction. Both of us were overwhelmed at the massiveness of the antlers that sat atop the head of the giant bull.

It was tough to concentrate on mule deer the rest of the day. All I could think about was the incredible bull, hoping he would still be around when the season opened. It would be a long week to wait.

I was born in Wyoming and started hunting when I was 12 years old. At age 49, when I spotted the trophy elk, I still hadn't taken a really big bull, and I had always wanted a chance at one of the monsters that now and then appear in the mountains where I do most of my hunting.

Because my wife is also an avid hunter, she accompanies me on most hunts. Often she'd draw a cow elk tag, and when she'd get her cow, I'd quit hunting elk and try for a big buck muley. One elk in the freezer would be enough meat for the year.

On November 18, 1991, I left my pickup and headed up the mountain, my flashlight showing the way. Opening day had finally arrived, and with it the chance of seeing the huge bull again. This time, however, I had an elk tag in my pocket and a dream in my heart.

It was snowing lightly, and the foot of snow on the ground made for tough walking. As darkness brightened into sunrise, the intensity of the storm picked up, and I was floundering about in a full-blown blizzard. Visibility was reduced to less than 100 yards. The arctic wind tore at me and my clothes were wet, and I realized that I could easily get into trouble with hypothermia. I reluctantly headed back to camp at about 9 a.m. to wait out the storm.

I was hunting the Sunlight Basin area northwest of Cody, Wyoming. The region is prime country that supports excellent elk populations, including the occasional transients that drift out of Yellowstone National Park, about 25 miles to the west.

After getting into dry clothes and cooking a hot lunch, I anxiously waited for the blizzard to break. Around noon the wind and snow let up, and the skies began to clear. I eagerly headed for the mountain again, but this time I decided to hunt lower than I'd originally planned. Heavy snow up on the ridges made travel all but impossible.

I chained up all four tires of my pickup and drove as far as I could. I left the rig at 2 p.m., bringing with me fresh batteries for my flash-light, waterproof matches and several candy bars. My destination was a series of drainages that had good cover and plenty of grass, as I knew that both of these elements are important to elk in snowy landscapes.

Later in the afternoon, while slowly moving along in the deep snow, I was shocked to see the huge bull. He was on the other side of a steep canyon—a canyon whose sides were too steep to climb down and too far apart to shoot across. I'd have to hike to the head of the drainage, cross it, and walk down the other side toward the bull. I looked at my watch and noted that I had only 1½ hours to make the stalk.

About an hour later, I eased out on a shelf above where the bull had been. To my dismay, the elk was gone. All I saw were tracks in the snow where the animal had been feeding.

With darkness coming fast, I had to make an important decision. Should I follow the bull and risk spooking him—if I hadn't already done so—or should I head back to the truck and try for the bull the next day? I knew that if I flushed the bull, darkness could end the day's hunt before I could find him again.

I knew that it would mean a long climb back to the truck—and much of it in the dark—but I had to know which direction the bull had gone.

Slipping up to the track, I discovered that two bulls had been feeding in the spot, not just the lone giant. Closer inspection revealed that the bulls had moved off in the opposite direction from the one I had figured.

I immediately followed the tracks.

Though daylight was fading, I forced myself to go slow and easy. At one point I eased up onto a small rise that had blocked my view and saw movement in the trail directly in front of me. Instantly I recognized the great bull as he raised his head and looked directly at me. He was less than 50 yards away!

With my heart beating wildly, I shouldered my .270 Weatherby Magnum and fired into the bull's lungs. The huge elk flinched but stayed on his feet. I knew that the bull was hit hard, but I wanted to get a second shot into him just in case. Unfortunately, he had taken a step, and now offered a poor target.

I was as excited as I'd ever been while hunting. I started telling myself to calm down. Finally the bull took another step—just enough for me to score another hit in the chest. By the time I chambered a third round, the mortally wounded bull had turned, and he now offered a full broadside shot. Taking no chances, I shot the bull through the top of the shoulders and put him down for good.

I was beside myself with excitement. I couldn't believe the size of the huge elk lying in the snow, and I shouted my joy into the forests around me. A lifetime dream had become reality.

My little victory celebration was short-lived, however, because I had just a few minutes of light to dress the bull. Then with the chore completed, I headed back to the truck in the dark.

Two hours later, my flashlight beam finally shone on the welcome sight of my truck. I drove home to Powell, Wyoming, with the thought of finding a pal to help get the elk out the next day.

As soon as I got home, I recounted the story to my wife and then called Harold Liner.

"Did you get him?" Harold, asked excitedly when he recognized my voice jabbering on the phone.

"I got him," I said, "but I need help getting him out. He's about a mile in."

"Is he as big as we originally thought?" Harold asked.

"I think he's bigger," I answered.

Harold immediately made arrangements to get the next day off from work, and the following morning, Harold, his younger brother, Danny, and I went in for the bull. We were equipped with pack-boards, ropes and a block and tackle.

We reached the bull just at dawn and had the elk to the truck about six hours later. We drove to Jim Marsico's Taxidermy Shop in Powell, and I asked Jim to take a look at the bull I'd killed.

As we headed out the door, I jokingly asked Jim if the bull was big enough to mount. But when Jim saw the bull, he just stood there in awe and stared. Finally he broke out of his trance, ran into his shop, produced a tape and measured the bull.

Jim is not an official scorer, but he is familiar with the scoring system, and when the elk taped out at 418 7/8 Boone and Crockett Club points, it astounded all of the people who had gathered to watch. (An official Boone and Crockett scorer measured the bull at 412 2/8 after drying.)

My bull will go down in history as the third-biggest elk ever killed in Wyoming—the best in the more than a century since the top two were taken. Not only that, but the official score puts the trophy at number eight in the world!

What makes the bull even more special is the fact that I took him on public land and didn't need to spend a lot of money hunting an expensive place that has a reputation for producing big bulls. I did it by first drawing a late season elk tag in an area outside Yellowstone Park that is known for giving up huge bulls, then by fortunately spotting the bull that I wanted and hunting exclusively for him.

Thanks to help from the weather that caused the bull to migrate, I finally have a bull for my wall.

And what a bull he is.

Outdoor Life, June 1992

Beat the Heat Bulls

BY LARRY D. JONES

In the initial stages of elk season, bulls can be bugling one hour and listless the next. Here are a few tricks you can use to crank up the heat on hot-weather bulls.

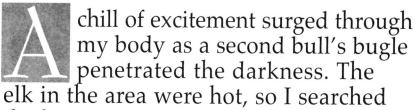 chill of excitement surged through my body as a second bull's bugle penetrated the darkness. The elk in the area were hot, so I searched the hillside for a flat spot to set up a bivouac camp.

Finding a small depression near a tree, I leveled a spot for my pad and sleeping bag by scraping pine cones and sticks aside. I checked broadheads for sharpness and readied my pack for the next morning's hunt. Satisfied that my equipment was organized, I slid into my sleeping bag. As I lay there that night in New Mexico, I was mesmerized by the sounds of chirping crickets, bugling bulls and the occasional hoot of an owl.

I was up and ready to hunt as the first rays of light silhouetted the branches of tall firs. Anxious to hear a bull's bugle, I used my metal reed call to pierce the stillness with loud bugles and pleading cow calls. From the depths of the timbered canyon, three bulls answered my challenge.

For two hours I bugled and pursued the bulls to pressure them. The chase led me to a trail that, according to my maps and boundary description, was the northern edge of my unit. I was close to the bulls, but even if I called them within shooting distance, I couldn't legally take one here. I decided to angle away from the trail by contouring around the hill. Two hundred yards inside the boundary I located a group of small, bushy firs. The spot would allow me to see approaching bulls while giving me necessary concealment. I slipped off my pack, nocked an arrow, leaned my bow against a tree and laid my camera on my pack. I bugled several times, carefully listening for a bull's response between calls. Not hearing any, I made a few cow calls, but still received no answer. I knew that there were bulls within hearing range, so I decided to call more aggressively.

For the next 30 minutes I used several different-sounding calls to produce bugles, grunts and cow calls. Elk are surprisingly vocal animals, so I varied the sounds of each challenge with growls, moans, squeals and rusty-gate-sounding screeches. I created demanding bugles followed by soft and loud cow mews and occasional whines to simulate a bull with his herd. Between each series of calls, I sat motionless and alert to any sound of an approaching bull.

Forty minutes into my attempts, I heard a branch snap. I quickly grabbed my bow as I stood to scan the timber. I didn't see anything, so I made two soft cow calls. Through an opening in the timber I saw a tan flash as a five-point bull trotted through. He leaped up a steep bank and took a course that would cross the path I had taken earlier.

He slowed to a walk and occasionally dropped his nose to sniff for hints of other elk. Suddenly, he stopped as he crossed my scent trail 30 yards away. He tested the air nervously, and I knew that he was about to retreat. I wished I had my camera in hand, because I didn't want to shoot this bull. Not only was this the first day of my hunt, but it was also three miles to a road, and the hot days and warm nights could cause meat spoilage by the time I packed out the animal.

Finally convinced that danger might be near, the bull turned and trotted back the way he had come. Once he was out of sight, I eased over to grab my camera, then made a couple of soft cow calls. I knew that it would be difficult to call him back, but through the trees I could see him sneaking toward me. He was suspicious, so he circled around me and never stood in the open. The few photos I took were of antlers in the brush.

This hunt was typical of many of my early season hunts. The days were sometimes sizzling hot and the nights were also warm. Hot weather can create more than one problem for elk hunters—the animals are less active, and it can be difficult to call them. Tracking an animal that's been hit can be tough because blood sign dries quickly, and the hard, dry ground doesn't show hoof prints. Meat spoilage can be a problem as well because the elk's thick hide and massive body retains heat. But after three decades of elk hunting, I've learned a few techniques to combat these problems.

Hot-Weather Hunting Methods

Hunting from tree and ground stands near water, wallows or feed areas can be excellent alternatives to calling, but scouting for the best spot is essential. When the weather is hot, your most promising feature is water. Find out which areas the elk are using. Once you discover a spot with plenty of sign, set up a blind or tree stand where you can get a shot when an elk passes.

Consider wind direction when selecting your ambush spot. Keep in mind the direction from which the elk will approach. Be sure that the wind is blowing from the elk to you. Construct your stand or blind so that you'll have shooting lanes that allow a broadside or quartering-away shot angle. Once in your blind, position yourself in the shadows. Elk have excellent eyesight.

Calling Methods

Some of the most successful tricks I've used to call elk during hot weather include calling before daylight, aggressive calling and using cow calls near bedding areas, water holes and wallows.

Bulls tend to be more active at night, so drive roads or walk trails an hour before daylight and call in different areas. Once you locate a bull, move within a few hundred yards and call again at first legal shooting light. You'll have a better chance of bringing a bull within range if you excite him before dawn and close in before the temperature rises.

If you have an idea where elk are bedding, approach their bedding area from downwind, but don't penetrate their bedding sites. Select a spot in the shadows where you'll have shooting lanes and where you could see a bull approaching. Use a cow call or mouth diaphragm call to produce a series of soft pleading mews. Make six to 12 mews, then listen for a mew or bugle. Continue this series for up to one hour. If you don't hear or see any bulls, move to another location and try again. Be persistent, and you can call bulls from their beds even on a sizzling hot day.

John West of Monroe, Michigan, hunted elk with me in Arizona a few years ago. We noticed that the majority of the hunters returned to camp every day around 10 a.m. because of the heat. West and I were confident we could call in bulls throughout the day, so we continued to hunt.

Early one afternoon, West was slowly stillhunting downwind of a bedding area when the strong, musky odor of elk whacked him in the nose. He selected a cluster of small trees to conceal himself and produced soft cow calls with a diaphragm. Within seconds he called a 6x6 bull to within 18 yards, but he didn't have a clear shooting lane. Once his heart quit pounding, he checked his watch: 12:30 p.m.

On another hot day an elk answered my pleading mews. West and I set up, and after 15 minutes of calling, a 4x4 bull walked to within 30 yards. We both wanted a bigger bull, so we let him walk away without attempting to shoot. I wanted to photograph the bull, so we circled and I sat in the shade of a cedar as West cow called from a cluster of pines. After 10 minutes, the four-point approached cautiously. I snapped four photos before the sound of my motor-driven camera sent the bull galloping into the protection of the trees.

Although a few subtle cow calls finessed that bull into camera range, some situations call for more aggressive tactics. On days when the bulls are unresponsive, I spend much of my time walking, calling and looking for sign. When I spot fresh tracks, droppings, rubs or wallows, I know that elk are nearby yet unwilling to answer my calls. In this situation, I use a combination of patience and aggressive calling to stir up some action.

I start by calling and listening, and I continue this sequence for up to one hour. I build a tempo of excitement through bugling, grunting, cow calling and scraping a tree with a stick, which sounds like a bull rubbing his antlers. I change calls often to sound like different elk. Bulls are lazy when it's hot, and they prefer to relax in the coolness of a shaded bed. Sometimes the excitement created through extended aggressive calling will arouse a bull to stand up and answer.

I've also called from a tree or blind at a water hole or a wallow. I prefer to use cow calls, but bugling will also work. I successfully used cow calls at a water hole one evening for one of the most exciting elk hunts I've ever experienced.

After being in my ground blind for 30 minutes, I made two series of cow calls. Shortly after the second series, a bull walked from the timber and approached the pond. His right antler had five points, but the left antler was broken above the first brow tine. He walked into the water and began to paw and splash water with his foot.

He lowered his head and began whipping it back and forth. His antler sent sprays of water right and left, splattering showers up to 20 feet away. As he stopped to look around, water streamed from his long chocolate-colored mane. He tore at the water again and then began jumping and bucking, sending mud and water flying. He twisted and stumbled and almost fell as he frolicked.

I was spellbound as I watched. After a while I decided to practice

TRACKING IN HOT WEATHER

A FEW IDEAS TO HELP YOU TRACK YOUR BULL ONCE HE'S HIT INCLUDE PAYING ATTENTION TO THE LENGTH OF HIS STRIDE, THE SHAPE OF HIS TRACK AND THE WAY THE BULL IS GROUPING HIS FEET.

Observe the way the bull places his feet or the shape of his hoof print–anything that makes his track unique. The feet of every bull have their own peculiarities. They may be round, pointed, have spread-out toes or a chunk missing from a hoof, but when they're shot they may favor one leg and leave a cluster of three tracks with one foot gouging the earth. When you find this, you can pick out the bull's track from others. Always follow tracks and identify blood sign to confirm that you're on the right track.

Where the bull has slowed to a walk, measure the length of his stride. It's helpful to know his stride when you can't find the next track or when you have to identify the bull's tracks among others. Use a stick, string or arrow to measure the stride. Lay the end of your measuring stick at the front of one tract and mark the stick where it hits the next track.

When you have a hard time finding the next track, place your stick at the front of the last known track and angle it in the direction where the next track should be. There should be a scuff mark or indentation very close to your stride mark. If the bull has turned, all you have to do is swing the stick around to the right or left to discover the next track.

drawing my bow on this foolish bull. I drew three times before remembering my camera. I eased it from my pack, but he quit his Walt Disney act before I could capture it on film. He sloshed across the pond and onto the bank, where I photographed him as he thrashed a bush.

After he left the area, I cow called again. After three or four series, another 5x5 bull approached. He walked into the pond and stood broadside, drinking. The beams and tines of his antlers were long. I was tempted to shoot, but I had my heart set on a 6x6. I let him melt into the trees before pleading with a few more cow calls.

This time a smaller bull came trotting into the pond. He wasn't cautious at all. Without hesitation, he splashed knee-deep into the pond, dropped to his belly and rolled. His legs went flying as water splashed onto his back. After several water-splashing rolls, he stood

HOT-WEATHER MEAT CARE

SOME OF THE CRITICAL FACTORS IN MEAT CARE START BEFORE YOU SHOOT, ESPECIALLY IN HOT WEATHER. AN ELK IS A HUGE ANIMAL. DON'T TAKE A SHOT SO FAR FROM CAMP OR IN SUCH RUGGED TERRAIN THAT YOU CAN'T REASONABLY PACK OUT THE MEAT BEFORE IT SPOILS.

Shot selection is also critical. The last hour of daylight can be one of the best times to excite a bull into range, but it's essential to make an excellent shot, especially in the heat. If you can't recover your trophy that evening, the meat may spoil. Therefore, limit your shot selection: Only shoot if you're within 20 yards with the elk broadside or slightly quartering away. Aim for the lower third of the body just behind the front leg hairline; that should put your arrow through both lungs so that the animal expires within seconds.

Once you find your trophy, it's extremely important to cool the meat as soon as possible. This is best accomplished by skinning your elk, removing the meat from the bones and laying it on branches so that air can flow around it. The meat's mass and large bones retain heat, so don't stack the meat into piles or it may spoil even after skinning.

A bull I killed while filming a video in Oregon was a good example of this. I wanted and walked from the pond with water drizzling from his drenched, mud-coated body.

Cow calls worked great from my blind that evening, to say the least, and the experience was the most eventful and fun I've ever had calling elk. Although you can't expect this kind of action every time you blow a call, hot-weather elk can be seduced if you make the right moves, set up in the best areas and make the correct calls.

Don't let hot weather spoil your hunt. Be prepared. Carry food and water so that you can continue to hunt when others return to camp. Adjust your attitude and hunting techniques. Use elk calls throughout the day and use aggressive calling to stimulate rutting bulls. Keep a step ahead of the elk—and the weather—and you can get into some sizzling hot excitement.

Outdoor Life, September 1992

to bone the animal on camera the following morning, so I gutted and skinned him and left his carcass lying on a tarp overnight. There was frost on the grass the next day, so I knew that the temperature had been below freezing that night. But when I stuck a meat thermometer into the neck meat, it registered more than 70°. Even without the thick hide, the sheer mass of the meat and large bones had retained heat.

If you experience sizzling hot days and night temperatures that never dip below 50°, you should get your meat to a freezer within 3 days.

One way to cool your meat if you can't get it to a locker is to quarter the elk and put the meat into a cool, fast-moving creek. Once the meat has cooled, hang it in the cool shade and dry it. Cover your meat with lightweight, fine-knit bags to protect it from dirt and blowflies. Each evening, remove the bags, separate the meat and place it in an open meadow where it can become as cool as possible during the night. Each morning re-bag it, place it in the shade and wrap it in sleeping bags. This insulates it from the heat of the day. This process requires some time and effort, but your meat can be stored for a week this way without spoiling.

Now Hear This!

BY JIM ZUMBO

The message hidden in that bugling can be fearful or fierce . . . so listen up, because it tells you how to hunt that bull.

The Selway Wilderness is quiet, except for the muted sounds of a creek somewhere in the distance. It's September 25, prime time for elk to be calling, but we hear absolutely nothing. It's one of those inexplicable times when elk fall silent. As I like to say, they're having a serious case of lockjaw.

We're doing everything we're supposed to do on a backwoods elk hunt. My guide and I are in the saddle at least an hour before the first glow of light in the eastern sky. Riding through total blackness, we hear nothing in the forest as each day is born, other than the barking of irritated red squirrels and hungry ravens squawking in the timbered canopy of huge firs and spruce above us.

This part of Idaho is no place for the hunter who likes seeing elk in the lovely parks and meadows, because there are none. The vast Selway is the most challenging chunk of elk country I've been in. Every time I go there I say I'll never go back, but I know down deep I don't really mean it. There's something about this busted-up, steep, blowdown jungle that keeps me returning for more.

BULL ELK will mark their territory with rubs. The hunter that finds these rubs and then calls from nearby is often successful.

So here we are, tying our horses to trees on a small ridge and descending into the bowels of a valley so heavily timbered you'd take bets that no elk could possibly move around. Yet you see piles of droppings here and there, and the occasional freshly rubbed tree spurs you on.

My guide, born and raised in elk country, is as drawn to the Selway as I am. I note early on that he bugles infrequently, maybe two or three times each morning. Opinions vary on elk calling, and my approach is always an aggressive one. Rather than being timid, I like to sound off regularly.

It's frustrating as we walk and ride through prime country without bugling. But I say nothing, out of respect for the guide. When we slip through heavy forest that breaks away into a fairly open stand of lodgepole pine and I see three deeply gashed saplings, I can stand it no longer. I know these slender trees were rubbed by a rut-crazed bull, and I sense we're in the bull's backyard. It's the perfect place to make a call, yet my guide continues on, unimpressed.

Resorting to trickery, I ask him to pose for my camera next to a photogenic snag that sprouts orange and yellow branches. I ask him to put the bugle up to his mouth. He does . . . but he doesn't blow into the call.

So I request that he belt out a bugle, saying his cheeks will be properly puffed up for an authentic-looking photo. He does, and what happens next will never dim in my mind.

A maddened scream tears out of the timber just 75 yards away. I dive for my rifle, which I'd put down in order to take the photos. The bull is coming straight at us, so close I can see his red nostrils flaring and his urine dribbling onto the forest floor as he searches for the intruder. He cocks his head, opens his mouth and rips off another lusty bugle, followed by whines and grunts. He is mad—outraged that another bull should enter his domain.

Moments later, my .30/06 cracks. The bull runs 60 yards and falls. He is a lovely animal, with impressive six-point antlers that will score 320 Boone and Crockett points.

A lesson is learned here. My guide called into this drainage half an hour earlier. We had been up on the ridge, the air was calm and the bull was within easy hearing distance. Yet he did not bugle back.

Call from His Backyard

During the breeding season, bulls set up territories, often marked by rubs. As demonstrated during this hunt, a bull will commonly ignore calls unless they're made from a location very close to or within what he considers his territory. Here is where many hunters err. It's easy to call from trails, roadways or other accessible places. Elk may fail to respond because: 1) they're alerted to those human traffic thoroughfares, or 2) the caller poses no threat to the bull's lair.

A bull's territory isn't necessarily a patch of landscape that he never leaves. It may be wherever he happens to be at the particular moment you enter his world. Solo bulls often rove about seeking cows, and herd bulls may drift along with their harem. In either case, I've found that bulls seem to draw their territorial boundary line at about 200 yards. If you get within that magic circle, odds are good that your bugling will draw in an irate audience.

Know When to Call

If, like my guide, you don't call much, you run the obvious risk of walking by a bull that would otherwise have responded had you called. On the other hand, if your calling is just part of a chorus made up of other hunters, too much calling may work against you. Even when they don't respond, bulls hear the excessive vocalization, and if they associate that bugling with humans, you can practically ensure the quarry's negative response.

If you're in the woods and hear other man-made bugling, try blowing a cow call softly. Of course, be aware that other hunters may hear your calls and come looking for you. Use good judgment when other hunters are about, and always wear hunter orange if you're hunting with a firearm, even if the state you're hunting in doesn't require it.

Calling is most effective at the edges of shooting light in the morning and afternoon. Be deep in the woods, and as far away from other hunters as you can get, even if this means traveling in the dark.

When He Stays Put

Perhaps the most exasperating aspect of elk hunting is the standoff— a stalemate in which neither side moves. Here's the scenario: Your bugle calls are answered with eager responses, but the bull won't budge.

Some hunters think this happens because the bull knows you're there. I don't believe it. If a bull knows you're there, he's history, and he wastes no time heading over the back ridge instead of talking back to you. Instead, this situation is most often caused by a bull's reluctance to make the final commitment to invade your space. To do so means a serious challenge.

Tempting this bull closer requires that you play some brain games. Stay silent for 10 or 15 minutes, and then softly blow a cow call. Make no more bugle sounds, but continue the cow calling. Be ever watchful, because this bull may sneak in. He's already heard you bugle, and now he hears only a cow. Because he doesn't know if another bull is present any longer, he's apt to slip in for a cautious look.

Another strategy to try when he hangs up is the "I'm tougher than you" routine. Break a branch with a loud snap and rake it noisily against a tree. Grab a nearby sapling and shake it hard. Bugle as you're going through these antics. You're telling the bull you're the meanest SOB in the valley. For this to work, you must be dealing with a bull that's in a mean mood. Again, be aware that he may come in quietly, but in this case he's more apt to rush in with hostile intentions. If, however, he's in an intimidated mood, you'll run him off, but that's the chance you take.

Some bulls refuse to come to any ruse. I once messed with a bull for a week, trying every trick and approach known to man. I called him

"Old Whistler," and he lived in a dense blowdown in the midst of a spruce forest. He wouldn't leave his hideout, no matter what. At one point, I slipped into the blowdown, using the sweetest cow call you ever heard, but still no dice. I think this was an old bull who had seen it all, and was no longer interested in fighting or romancing: Been there, done that, now just leave me alone.

When He Retreats

If you've been there and done that, you'll know how frustrating it is to talk to a bull only to have him run away for no apparent reason. Your initial reaction will probably be to blame yourself, assume you're making bad calls or figure he's wise to you. Not necessarily so. There are two types of bulls you might be dealing with, and each has a perfectly natural reason to run away.

• The Harem Master or Herd Bull: This bull has already gathered a harem of cows, and his object in life is to keep them in his possession until he breeds them all. Many forces are at work to thwart this goal. The bull must sometimes round up his wandering cows by brandishing his antlers. Or he may have to rush cows who decide simply to walk away—a cow may want out of the party because she doesn't care much for the host, or she hears another bull who sounds more interesting. Then, of course, the herd bull must deal with other bulls who want to share his prizes. If the harem master is aggressive, he

STOPPING A SPOOKED ELK

THIS AMAZING TECHNIQUE WORKS LIKE A CHARM. ALL IT TAKES IS A COW CALL AND THE CONFIDENCE TO USE IT.

When an elk, or herd of elk, is running away, blow your cow call sharply, as loud as you can. Be prepared for a shot, because the elk are likely to stop and look back. Wear your call around your neck so it's handy when you need it. Trust me, this strategy is remarkably effective. Most hunters haven't tried it because the last thing you do when elk are fleeing is think to blow a call. Instead, you're jockeying for a shot. Be a believer and blow the call.

will streak out to challenge an intruder, but if he's insecure about his place in the hierarchy of the woods, he may simply run his cows off, away from the bugling challenger.

So there you are, blowing your world-class bugle call flawlessly, just like the experts, but your dream bull is running away from you. Take heart in realizing that even a real bull cannot turn this fleeing one. It's time to think romance instead of war. Put the bugle call away and begin a sweet melody of cow chirps. Be ready for action, because your chicken-hearted bull may stop in his tracks, leave his cows and rush down to check out the newest lady elk in the woods.

• The Satellite Bull: Most commonly this is a youngster who wears four or five points to the side and is no match for the harem master. However, other solo bulls are old-timers who own impressive racks but are no longer physically able to compete with stronger, dominant bulls. The two types of loner bulls have one thing in common: They have no cows and are unhappy with that lot in life. If they hear another bugle, chances are they won't respond in aggressive fashion. They may bugle back, but that's it, or they may sneak in to see if any loose cows are with the bull they hear, taking pains to stay a safe distance away. More commonly, they'll retreat. As subdominant bulls, they don't want to risk clashing with Mr. Big. The same holds for the solo bull past his prime. He's also unwilling to skirmish.

The solution? Use the cow call. Logic tells you that single bulls want company. Make them think you're just the company they're seeking. I'm such a firm believer in the cow call that I seldom use a bugle call at all. For me, the cow call does it all.

Timing the Rut Cycle

In the summer, bulls hang out in bachelor groups, putting on weight rapidly and growing antlers encased in velvet. The velvet sheath peels off in the August prerut, and bulls begin looking for cows. Some archery seasons open in late August and very early September, during this prerut. If you're having trouble getting bulls to respond to calling, try setting up over wallows—they're often visited on a daily basis, and elk usually visit a wallow via a well-used trail. A tree stand or ground blind downwind of the trail is ideal.

Elk are polygamous animals, as are all other members of the deer family. But unlike buck deer, bulls are in steady contact with females. Keeping the cows in a tight herd is a 24-hour-a-day job, and bulls are constantly trying to retain the cows and attempting to win more. By September 20 or so, the rut reaches a frenzy, with bulls tearing about wildly, looking for cows. Much activity occurs between bulls as they establish dominance. Most commonly, two bulls will approach each other, bugle wildly and demolish saplings with their antlers. The bluffing continues until one of the bulls runs off or it escalates. Antler-sparring is the ultimate challenge. This is no lightweight shoving contest. It's a duel with 700-pound bodies savaging each other accompanied by a great deal of noise, dust and, sometimes, blood.

Yet amid all this noise and fury, there are times when bugling may be suppressed by weather, such as damp, rainy periods or exceptionally hot weather. If bugling becomes infrequent, don't think that breeding has stopped. Not at all. It continues, even though vocalization halts. Continue calling as usual, but expect silent approaches by responding bulls.

As the breeding season winds down in early October, harems begin breaking up, and bulls focus on cows that haven't yet been bred. Although activity isn't as frantic as during the peak of the rut, bulls remain very much in the breeding mode, and will continue to respond to calling. If you hear bugling in late October or even November or December, you're probably hearing a bull sounding off at a cow that wasn't bred during the rut, but has come back in heat again. These bulls seldom respond to calling.

THE AUTHOR consistently takes big bulls by knowing where, when and how to call.

Outdoor Life, October 1997

Alaska Moose

BY JIM ZUMBO

Finding an animal out in the woods that's as big as a pickup should be easy ... not!

Smoke hangs heavy in the bar as Willie Nelson sings a sad song on the jukebox. Patrons sit quietly, sipping beers and watching a football game on television. This could be any bar in America, but for me it's new—and unique. I'm in Alaska, a state that leaves me awed by everything I see. People, trees, rocks, water—every aspect of this amazing land commands respect. I never tire of it, no matter how many times I visit. Each trip generates a fresh excitement.

An old man in a dark corner catches my eye as I look for a place to sit. Normally I don't react to strangers, but I'm drawn to him without reservation as he waves me over. He appears to be in his 80s, but I suspect he's closer to my age—somewhere in his mid-50s. Two or three teeth are the sum total of his dental assets; his high cheekbones and dark eyes betray his ancestry. I peg him as a native Alaskan, which proves to be correct.

He asks me if I'm from "outside," a term meaning non-Alaskan, and I tell him I'm from Wyoming, that I'm here to hunt moose. His eyes light up when I mention moose, and he launches into a discussion of the big animals, starting with his first experience with them at age five. I sit enthralled, listening to this man who lives a life that few in mainstream America could comprehend.

People of the North fascinate me. Unlike natives of the Tropics, who live in a nearly optimal climate, northern natives are not so fortunate. Bitterly cold weather and dark winters with fleeting glimpses of a frigid sun are facts of life, as is the bug-ridden summer that comes and goes too quickly.

I'm mildly disappointed when the barmaid pages me. My hunting pals, Jack Atcheson Sr. and a friend of his, have arrived. It's time to prepare for our trip into the bush. Reluctantly, I bid my new pal farewell, eager to begin my newest Alaskan adventure.

Atcheson is one of my favorite hunting partners. He is real—a guy who doesn't know the meaning of the word "quit," and someone who savors the hunt more than anyone else I know. I grew up reading about Atcheson's adventures with Jack O'Connor, and later with Jim Carmichel. Almost 20 years ago, I finally met the legendary man, and we hit it off. This Alaska hunt would be about the 10th we've experienced together. At 67, Jack has been through two bypass surgeries, but you'd never know it. Like I said, he's no quitter.

Atcheson tells me that he's hunted Alaska moose maybe 15 times, give or take a time or two. As a former booking agent from Butte, Mont. (he recently retired and his sons Jack Jr. and Keith now run the business), he hunts as much as ever around the world, but moose are a favorite.

We will be accompanied on this hunt by Doug Kennemore, a neurosurgeon from South Carolina and a good hunting buddy of Jack's. I'm anxious to meet Doug. In the world of non-hunters, we're often accused of being a bunch of beer-swilling rednecks. I'm always tickled to hunt with a guy who has the brains of, well, a neurosurgeon. Doug turns out to be a great guy. I'm also anxious to meet Henry Budney, an old pal of Jack's.

As it turns out, Henry, a Connecticut industrialist, owns a chunk of real estate in Alaska, and we'll be hunting it, with Fred Sorenson, an outfitter who runs the hunts. Fred lives in the Alaska bush, where he offers outstanding fishing trips for salmon in the summer. Now then, if you think rural Alaska equates with the outback of Mississippi or a West Virginia hollow, you're not even close. Fred's part of the world is serviced exclusively by airplane—a place where such basics as mail, grocery stores and doctors are a long flight away. During bad weather, there are no flights; you grin and bear it.

In Alaska, avid outdoorsmen don't buy only pickup trucks—they buy airplanes, too. The relatively few roads are hammered by hunters. Generally speaking, if you want a big moose, you fly, pure and simple.

All of us want big moose, which is why Jack arranged the hunt with Fred. His area comprises rugged tundra and spruce country, and it's very remote. Like other game animals, a bull moose gets big because he gets old. To get old, the bull has to live in an area with little or no hunting pressure. Fred's area provides that. Everything about a moose is big—from his nose to his body mass to his antlers.

Everyone who hunts Alaska bulls has a fantasy about shooting a moose with a 70-inch spread. So do we, but Jack gives us a reality check.

"I'd estimate one out of 500 bull moose has a 70-inch spread," Atcheson says, drawing upon his wide experience as a hunter and former taxidermist. "Most people think all you have to do is get away from roads, usually via an airplane, and your 70-incher is waiting. In my experience, the average mature Alaskan moose has an outside spread of between 53 and 55 inches."

My sights are set on a mature bull, whether it's 50 or 60 inches. Of course, bigger is always better, but I won't be disappointed if the Bull of the Woods doesn't show up. Just being in the Alaska wilderness is reward enough for me.

We're flown into camp by Art Ward, a bush pilot who ferries us in one at a time in his Piper Super Cub. The little airplane is a requirement for this mission because the landing spot is a rough-and-tumble strip of tundra pockmarked with hummocks and potholes.

Camp includes sleeping tents and a cook tent. Doug and I share one, while Jack and Henry move into the other. I soon learn that Henry, at 82, is without a doubt the most physically fit octogenarian I've ever met. This guy is a grad-school John Glenn, and would put most 40-year-old American males to shame in an endurance or hiking contest.

Henry has a unique conveyance in camp, a large Bombardier ATV on tracks. This ATV holds six people or more, and has all the appointments of an army tank. It will take you practically anywhere, provided you're willing to allow yourself to be beaten half to death as the thing bounces, lurches and rocks and rolls across the landscape. The rig remains in camp year-round. Fred uses the unit to ferry hunters from one camp to another, a distance of about 12 miles, as well as to travel to lookout spots miles away. Our plan is to ride in it before daybreak each morning to a point about six miles from camp, where we'll climb up a hill and glass for moose below. The vantage point allows a mile-long view. Once an acceptable bull is located, the rest of the hunt will be spot-and-stalk.

The plan for the first morning is for Jack and Henry to climb above camp and look for moose in open country broken by fingers of thick alder. Doug and I will ride with Fred to the base of the observation hill in the ATV, and hike high enough to where we can see the valley below.

By first light the next morning we've climbed far above the valley. The going is miserable. Soft spongy clumps of tundra make walking a grind. We finally settle into comfortable positions and begin glassing for big black objects in the vegetation below.

Within an hour we've spotted four bulls, but none wears antlers much over 50 inches. More glassing produces three more bulls, but still no big boys. We continue to observe from different positions on the mountain throughout the day. With darkness just a couple of hours away, we finally spot two outstanding bulls. They're in thick spruce about 100 yards apart, and a half-mile from us. Though they're easy to see from our elevated perch, I know they'll be almost impossible to spot once we're at ground level. We make a gallant effort, but the bulls are swallowed up in the dense forest.

We're back up on the hill before sunrise the next day, but the big bulls have evaporated in the trees. It's almost time for lunch when Fred spots one of the bulls, and again we head down the tundra slopes for another attempt.

This search is also unproductive, and at one point we meet Henry. He has walked six miles from camp to bring us the news that Jack has shot a good bull. Henry climbs up the slope to help us look, and I am again amazed at his ability to travel, despite his age.

Darkness is just an hour away as we slip along, looking for the moose. Suddenly I spot a very big bull headed directly toward us about 80 yards out.

I don't need a second opinion to tell me this is an animal to reckon with, so I quickly shoulder my Browning 7mm Remington Magnum, place the crosshairs behind the crease of his shoulder and squeeze the trigger.

The bull stumbles at the shot and lurches forward, and I shoot again, hitting him in the same spot. This time he staggers, trots 30 yards and sways unsteadily on his feet. A final bullet puts him down for good.

"What a bull," Fred says as we rush toward the fallen animal. "He's better than 60 inches."

The sight that greets me as I approach the moose is a memory never to be erased. This bull is as big as my pickup truck. His antlers have wide, tall palms, with heavy brow tines. His still-bloody antlers reveal he has just shed the velvet within the past few hours. We stretch a tape across the massive antlers and read 63 inches.

I walk around the moose six or seven times, completely taken by his size. His body is so much larger than any of the other moose I've taken that I can't believe it. (Of the three subspecies recognized by the Boone and Crockett Club, the Alaska-Yukon is the largest.) I have no way to tell, but I'd wager my bull weighs in excess of 1,500 pounds.

Two days later I leave camp, headed for home with a great set of antlers, an enormous cargo of meat and a bushelful of extra memories—like the grizzly that walked into camp, the huge wolf that I shot at and missed and the old man sitting in the dark bar.

Outdoor Life, March 1999

ALASKA ON YOUR OWN

General Information: Nonresident moose hunters are not required to hire a guide. Other than fully outfitted trips, two other popular hunts are drop-camps and float-trips.

Seasons: Alaska has 26 Game Management Units, each with different seasons. Generally moose season is in September, but call the Alaska Department of Fish and Game (907-465-4100) for specific regulations.

Get in Shape: If you don't hire an outfitter, the critical factor to consider is your physical condition. Field-processing a moose and transporting it are extremely strenuous activities. Don't try this if you aren't in good shape, unless you're accompanied by close friends who are willing to shoulder your share of the work.

Meat Care: If the weather is warm, make arrangements with your air taxi service to check on you periodically, if possible. Meat should be flown out soon after the kill is made to prevent spoilage.

Booking Hunts: To hunt with Fred Sorenson, call Atcheson Hunting Consultants (406-782-3498).

Caribou:
A Great Adventure

BY JIM ZUMBO

*Every minute spent in
the wilds of caribou
country is worth it.*

I watched in amazement as Gregg Severinson opened the tent flap a bit more for a better look at the hundreds of caribou that were streaming past. Big bulls trotted by just 50 yards from camp, and I knew sleep wouldn't come easy.

Because Alaska law doesn't allow you to hunt the same day you fly, we had to wait until morning. I wasn't worried, though, because our trip in had revealed an incredible sight. Our pilots flew along a huge herd of 30,000 caribou. They were traveling in a long line, just a few miles from the Alaskan coast.

The pilots put the planes down in a small, dry lake bed. We'd camp near the head of the herd. It would take days for the animals to file past, and unless something unexpected happened, this was as close to a guaranteed hunt as any I'd ever been on.

Gregg is manager of Cabela's Outdoor Adventures, a branch of the huge retail and catalog store that arranges hunts around the world (800-346-8747). The two of us had hunted together many times in the past. Gregg is a skilled outdoorsman and one of the best hunters I know—the kind of guy I like to make a drop-camp with.

A Perfect Hunt

Our Alaska camp had just the bare essentials, and when the pilots left us in their small Super Cubs, we were on our own. It would be a test of survival if the weather turned bad. I'd been in this area in the past and knew how quickly a storm could brew.

As it turned out, my worries were unfounded because the sun shone brightly and it was calm the next morning. Gregg and I had our caribou down before noon, but not until we saw hundreds of bulls. Mine was a dandy, with long, massive beams and plenty of tines, but Gregg's was a really good bull. So good, in fact, that he flew the antlers out whole so they could be scored for the Boone and Crockett record book. (We later learned that Gregg's bull just missed the book.) I cut mine in half so they'd stow more easily in the bush plane, a common practice in the North Country. (Splitting the antlers disqualifies them for entry in B&C.)

That hunt had been perfect: The weather cooperated, and we were camped near a massive migration. It was a storybook hunt, and other than packing meat to camp on backpacks, it wasn't much of a physical effort. My bull fell about 400 yards away; Gregg's was about twice that distance.

Caribou Quirks

Caribou are unique animals, unlike anything else I've ever hunted in North America. They typically gather in big herds, migrate long distances and live in the most remote country on the continent. Of all the caribou I've hunted, which includes four of the North American subspecies, all required an airplane flight into the backcountry. In addition, I've used horses, boats and canoes to reach herds once the planes got us to the base camp.

Another unique aspect of caribou is their wariness, or lack thereof. Any time someone tells me a caribou displayed a sense of intelligence toward humans, I have to wonder. Jack O'Connor, *Outdoor Life's* late Shooting Editor, referred to caribou as being somewhat stupid. "If they run away," O'Connor liked to say, "they usually forget what spooked them and run back for a closer look." I've seen them behave the same way on several of my hunts.

A few years ago, while I was hunting Dall sheep in Alaska, a bull caribou approached our horses as we rode up a riverbed.

The animal took one look at us, bolted and ran off smartly. Less than a minute later, the bull returned, ran up within 50 yards and stared at us as we rode. He followed us for a mile, completely at ease with our presence. Unfortunately, none of us had a caribou tag or it would have been a no-brainer hunt.

When hunting mountain caribou in British Columbia, our party rode horseback onto a snowy plateau. We spotted two herds of caribou, and I flipped a coin with another hunter in our group to decide which herd we'd pursue. One had a huge bull, and, as luck would have it, the other hunter won the coin toss.

Reggie Collingwood, my outfitter, and I rode close to the other herd. When we were 400 yards away they seemed to be getting nervous. Following Reggie's suggestion, we dismounted and walked toward the animals, leading our horses by their halters so we were just barely in front of the horses. The caribou calmed down and watched placidly as we came to within 150 yards, whereupon I lay prone in the snow, drew a bead on the bull and dropped him where he stood. Evidently the caribou were not at all concerned with the horses, and when we walked close to our animals we represented no danger. The other hunter, by the way, shot his bull easily and it scored high in the record book.

A believable theory has it that caribou are trusting because their remote habitat isolates them from humans. A person standing upright has no resemblance to the wolf, their primary predator, and most caribou never see a human during their entire lives.

The Real Challenge

In my estimation, the biggest challenge in caribou hunting is simply getting to hunting camp. I recall one trip where we had to take canoes 80 miles along the Arctic Ocean to reach caribou herds. Former *Outdoor Life* editor Vin Sparano and I made that trip, and once or twice I had doubts that we'd get out of there unscathed. We were guided by an Inuit who spoke broken English, and somehow we managed to get to the hunting area, though stormy seas forced us to take refuge on small rocky atolls. When we reached camp, half of the 18 hunters in our party quickly jumped out of the canoes with their rifles and shot their bulls within 200 yards of the beach. The rest of us waited, and within three days all of us had our bulls. None of those animals showed alarm at our presence.

Playing the Odds

Though there are plenty of "easy" hunt stories, there are nightmare hunts as well, and I'm not referring to weather-related problems only. Many caribou hunts are geared to migrations, and those are the ones most hunters complain about, if they indeed have complaints. Sometimes the migrations aren't timed with the hunters' presence, which means the hunt will be a bust, pure and

CARIBOU, because they are so plentiful throughout much of northern Canada and Alaska, provide hunters the trip of a lifetime without costing a small fortune.

simple. It doesn't matter how good a hunter you are, or how physically tough you are—if there isn't a living caribou within 50 miles of camp, you might as well fish or pop a ptarmigan or two. It happens every year, in dozens of camps in the North Country, even to reputable outfitters who have great track records.

Drop-camp hunts like the one Gregg and I went on are usually reliable because pilots know where the animals are and will set you down close by. In other parts of Alaska and across Canada, there are resident herds that provide hunting all fall in the same general areas. Hunting migrating animals can be a big gamble, as many disappointed hunters can attest to.

When you plan your caribou hunt, think adventure. The Far North has a special mystique, and you'll feel woefully inadequate when you enter this enormous, desolate landscape. Even though caribou might seem a bit lacking in the brain department, I'm betting you'll love every minute in their fascinating world.

Outdoor Life, September 1998

HORNED
GAME

The Great Pretender

BY MICHAEL PEARCE

Getting within bowhunting range of antelope requires a bit of fakery.

I had finally made it, the small, gnarled clump of sage that marked the end of my trail. I had walked, crawled, and finally slithered to where I could peek through the tiny bush and see the object of my stalk, still 200 yards away. The pronghorn buck was at the apex of a Wyoming ridge. But rather than hiding, he was boldly pacing back and forth in the soft, late afternoon light as he scanned the landscape in every direction.

It was a gimme shot for someone with a rifle, but with a compound bow at my side, I was stymied. If I tried to move closer, the buck, perched on the highest ground around, would spot me. And even if by some miracle he didn't, any one of his harem of half a dozen does surely would.

But as I watched, the buck peeled off his ridge, streaked past the does, and bore down upon me in a full-blown charge. I could see fury in his eyes as he closed the yards between us: 50, 40, 30, 20 . . . "Whoa!" I thought as I drew my bow. "All I wanted was a close shot, not a 'This Happened to Me' episode."

At one time archers were given the longest of hunting odds when they took to the prairies for pronghorns. The openness of the terrain and the antelope's eagle eyes often made for single-digit success rates. But about a decade ago, bowhunters began hunting from pit blinds, capitalizing on the pronghorn's dependence on water holes in an arid environment. And suddenly the odds went down.

But pit-blind hunting is not without drawbacks. A cloudburst can fill everything from tire ruts to buffalo wallows with water, devaluing established water holes as a drawing card for game. You also need the patience and personality of a monk to spend all day in a dank hole in the ground.

Don't get me wrong, a day spent reading Elmore Leonard's latest thriller while occasionally glassing distant pronghorns beats a day at work 10 times out of 10. Believe me, if a pit blind was the only way to take a good pronghorn, I'd spend more time in the ground than a prairie dog.

But now there is a better way to bowhunt antelopes. And, as a bonus, it's every bit as exciting as turkey calling or whitetail rattling—maybe even more so!

There's nothing new about bringing pronghorns into range of a bow. Native Americans were fond of tying feathers or bright cloth to bushes and waiting until an antelope's curiosity brought it in for a closer look. The pioneers later picked up on the idea. Fast-forward to the 1960s and '70s, when a few ingenious archers began using homemade decoys to bring in pronghorns. Decoying success rates have skyrocketed in recent years, thanks to some new twists introduced by Mel Dutton, a Faith, S.D., bowhunter.

"We originally used crude 3D decoys that we set up near bale blinds," says Dutton. "Sometimes a little herd buck or a smaller buck would come over to check it out. But it was pretty much just a waiting game, so I decided to take the decoy to the antelope."

Dutton soon learned that he'd have to make some changes if he wanted to spend more time hunting and less time waiting. "I tried carrying a big decoy to the antelope for two seasons, but the size of the thing made it so awkward during stalking that most of the time I'd spook the antelope before I got set up," he says. "And it sure wasn't much fun sneaking around long distances with that cumbersome thing."

After a great deal of trial and error Dutton came up with a jointed, plastic silhouette of a pronghorn that weighs about the same as an empty briefcase and carries just as easily. Though the decoy bears a resemblance to a pronghorn, you have to wonder if it could fool America's most keen-eyed mammal. Doubters should consider this: During three days while filming a show for ESPN in 1992, Dutton used one of his decoys to pull 20 different pronghorn bucks within easy bow range.

Such success is almost entirely credited to the gender of antelope the decoy represents. Rather than the predictable likeness of a doe, Dutton's decoy carries a pair of small, stubby horns to capitalize on a rare chink in the armor of a high-horned buck. Unlike rutting whitetails, which scamper about the countryside looking for solitary one-night stands, pronghorn bucks gather harems of up to 20 does. Once collected, the buck simply waits for his dates to reach estrus. It's a time of nearly nonstop activity for the bucks. They're constantly scanning the surrounding prairie looking for new does they can add to their herd and rounding up any errant females that may have strayed from the fold.

There is also the threat of smaller bucks, which desperately want in on the autumn ritual. These small-horned antelope regularly scout the herds looking for a chance to run off a straying female or even to move in and take a doe or two while the dominant buck is otherwise occupied. Big herd bucks show no patience with such interlopers and upon sighting them waste little time chasing them from the area. In fact, their loathing is so intense that it overcomes their wariness, and the bucks seldom take the time to check if the pronghorn is real or plastic, with an archer nestled in behind. For obvious reasons, decoying is NOT to be tried during firearms and muzzleloading seasons.

As with all game calling, there are techniques that add to the trickery. Hunters must take precautions against a pronghorn's legendary eyesight and underrated sense of smell. At the same time, a close setup is essential. "Though the buck will sometimes come from as far away as a quarter of a mile, it's best to get within 150 to 200 yards," says Dutton. "If you're too far out, he'll often just keep an eye on you, but if you set up close, he feels more threatened and is far more likely to try to run the little buck off. On the other hand, you don't want to overdo it and get so close that you spook him."

Timing is another crucial element. Unlike turkeys or bugling elk, which respond best early and late in the day, decoying antelope works well from dawn to dusk at the right time of year. "It works best just before the peak of the rut, when the bucks are working hard to gather does," says Dutton. "I mostly hunt the prairies of South Dakota and Wyoming, and the peak usually comes in the middle part of September. I have decoyed them as early as Sept. 2, but it's better a week or so later on."

According to Dutton, dominant herd bucks are hard to decoy when the rut is going strong because it's tough to draw their attention from breedable does and the satellite bucks. An archer's chances are best on a buck that's with a lone hot doe. As the rut begins to fade, a doe decoy will often pull in a big buck who is looking for his final fling of the season.

Dutton and other pronghorn decoying veterans all say it's a sport of mixed success. There are days when every buck tried will do little more than look at the silhouette. There will also be days when every buck comes into arrow range. Dutton considers it a disappointment if he doesn't get four or five bucks to come in during the peak of the rut.

The bucks that come do so in a variety of ways. Some simply trot straight toward the decoy in a straight line. Others take their time with lots of posturing and profiling, while the hunter's heart beats a rising rhythm as he mentally coaxes the buck closer. And if he's really lucky, an archer will happen across an antelope with an attitude.

The rut was just beginning when Bill Hines, of Pumpkin Buttes Outfitters in Gillette, Wyo., and I did some shopping before I first tried my hand at decoying. We spent several hours watching the constant action of bucks corralling does and chasing subdominant bucks. Then, toward evening, we spotted a band off by itself.

One look told us the buck carried the kind of horns we wanted, and even through the spotting scope he seemed to exude an attitude Mike Tyson would envy.

"Look around," said Hines. "This is the only herd of antelope in this part of the pasture. There aren't even any little bucks within sight. I'd say this bad boy's already run them off. It looks like he's ready to do it again."

As we watched the big pronghorn pace back and forth for a few minutes, I planned the stalk. I began my sneak by walking down a deep arroyo and ended it 500 yards later after I'd pushed the bow and the decoy to the top of a small ridge. When I saw that the buck was momentarily distracted by one of his does, I carefully unfolded the decoy, lifted it, and planted the stake in the

PRONGHORNS favor wide-open habitat, giving them an advantage over bowhunters, but correct use of a decoy can bring bucks within range.

ground in front of my prone body. Now hidden from view, I got to my knees and looked through the small peek hole. The buck was facing my way and taking short, nervous steps.

Earlier, Dutton had cautioned me to always be ready, so I quietly popped an arrow from the quiver and took a second look. The buck was trotting down the ridge toward me, leaving his does behind. I nocked the arrow with shaking fingers, slipped one hand around the bow, and secured my release with the other. Peering through the hole in the decoy for the third time, I saw that he was now at the bottom of the ridge and coming fast, wearing the look of a jealous husband.

Keeping my face down, I began in slow motion to rock back on my heels while slowly drawing the Golden Eagle I had spent hours tuning for this moment. To my relief, the buck slammed on the brakes at 15 yards. Perplexed, the pronghorn faded back to 30 yards, where he stopped and stared. I don't remember the release, just my 30-yard pin settling in behind the buck's front leg and the sound of a kill shot.

Hines and I found the buck a stone's throw away. With a matching pair of 15-inch horns that carried good prongs and mass, the buck green-scored over 80 Pope and Young points and should rank very high in the book.

Standing there admiring the antelope while the excitement of the hunt flashed through my mind, I realized I had gained a new hunting addiction.

Outdoor Life, August 1995

Pronghorn Savvy

BY MICHAEL HANBACK

A top guide reveals his favorite antelope tactics.

ithout taking his eye away from the spotting scope, Ric Martin drawled, "We'd better take a closer look at that one."

The buck antelope was standing alone in the sage, maybe a quarter-mile from the rest of his small herd. And although the animal was two coulees away, I could see the morning sunlight glinting on black horns through my 1OX binoculars.

"Let's go," Martin said in his southwestern twang. I loaded a few rounds into my .30/06 and headed out with him across the New Mexico plains.

Many guides like to sprint toward game, as if proving that their legs, lungs and resolve are stronger than yours. That is not Martin's style. He stalks antelope as if he's walking down a street in Albuquerque. His stride is smooth and steady. Just gliding over the open country, he exudes an air of confidence that rubs off on anyone who has come to the high plains in September for a crack at a trophy pronghorn.

A stalk after wild game is supposed to be filled with pressure and suspense. So why was I smiling? I thought back to the previous evening in the cook tent. Over cold beers and grilled steaks, Martin had regaled the crew with tales of exploits on six continents. For more than three decades he has climbed after sheep and elk, guided for Tanzanian lions and even stared down gun barrels at Cape buffalo and elephants.

Now he was ambling along and, all the while, easing me within rifle range of one of the smallest and daintiest big-game animals on the planet. It seemed a bit ironic.

But hunting the American pronghorn is serious business for Martin. The guy has a passion for the sport: You can see it in his eyes. After 30 minutes of easy stalking, he stopped, looked in my direction and then waved a finger toward the next draw. I shinnied up a rock ledge and sneaked a look. The buck was feeding right there—right where Martin had pointed.

I turned my riflescope up to 9X and centered the crosshairs. It was a fine animal, but was he 200, 300 or 500 yards away? It can be tough to tell on the featureless plains.

"He's exactly 312 yards," Martin whispered, reading my mind from behind his range finder. "You're shooting a 150-grain, right? Just hold on the hair on the very top of his back."

I took a deep breath, expelled half of it and pressed the trigger. Dust boiled on the opposite side of the buck. Had the bullet passed through, or had I blown it? The pronghorn answered by whirling and running off in a blur. "Shoot again," Martin said calmly.

I cranked the scope back to 4X and picked up the disappearing antelope. Confused, he stopped in a coulee. This time, I squeezed the trigger and hit the animal square behind the shoulder. He didn't run far.

THE PRONGHORN is similar to the gazelle of Mongolia. In the words of Ric Martin, who has hunted all over the world: "Both have phenomenal eyesight, and both run like the wind."

I am not one of those lucky souls who usually shoots something on the first day of a hunt. So when I do score from the get-go, you can bet I savor the moment. For the better part of an hour I admired that buck, one of my finest ever. His heavy, well-pronged horns taped 15½ inches and were wonderfully symmetrical, curving up and in to form the outline of a heart. Martin and I sat awhile, smelling the sage and enjoying the warm autumn sunshine and vastness of the plains.

"Let's talk antelope," I said. I'd known the man for less than a day, but we had just stalked and shot an awesome animal and, somewhere in the process, had connected as only hunters can. What better time to pick the brain of one of the Southwest's foremost pronghorn outfitters?

MICHAEL HANBACK: Why do you enjoy antelope hunting so much?

RIC MARTIN: When a shooting situation materializes, there's not as much pressure on the hunter to capitalize on that one opportunity as there is in hunting elk or sheep. Antelope are everywhere in their open habitat. Hunters can see 30 to 50 head a day, and 20 percent of those will be bucks. Those are conservative estimates. If you don't find a buck you like on the first day, or if you blow a shot, there are usually other opportunities.

MARTIN CAN BE CONTACTED for information about trophy antelope hunts by calling 505-829-3897.

Antelope hunting is also not that strenuous, either. It's good sport for all hunters, no matter what shape they're in.

MH: How does the American pronghorn compare to other game animals you've hunted and guided for around the world?

RM: The antelope reminds me a little of the impala. Both animals run in herds, and the male/female relationship is similar. There's usually a dominant buck with lots of females, and subordinate bucks hanging around the fringes of the herd.

Most antelope inhabit sprawling, short-grass plains. Occasionally you'll find bucks in foothills dotted with cedars or juniper. The springbok is like that. Most springbok live out in open savannas, but, like the prong-horn, sometimes you'll find animals living in higher, denser cover.

When I think of pronghorn antelope I also think of the whitetail gazelle of Mongolia. Both animals have phenomenal eyesight and both run like the wind, making them tough to stalk.

MH: Why are you so high on the pronghorn hunting here, in your home state?

RM: In terms of sheer numbers of antelope, New Mexico can't com-pare to, say, Wyoming or Montana. But this is big-buck country. We don't even look closely at a buck unless we figure his horns will go 14½ to 16 inches. We've shot several Boone and Crockett bucks on the ranches that we hunt, including a couple last season.

MH: While we're on the subject of big bucks, how do you field-judge those horns—what do you look for?

RM: You have to look not only for horn length, but also for good mass and high, nicely developed prongs. I've seen 17-inch bucks that wouldn't score nearly as well as antelope with heavy, well-pronged, 15½-inch horns.

MH: How important are your optics?

RM: You can't hunt the high plains effectively without a top-quality 8X or 10X binocular. You also need a high-magnification spotting scope for zeroing in on horns. And finally, you should top your rifle with the best scope you can afford.

I never hunt pronghorns without my Leica Geovid range finder around my neck. After three decades on the western plains and the Tanzanian savannas, I still find it hard to judge distances. Dialing in on a 100-pound antelope in big, treeless country is especially tough. I can't say enough about a laser range finder. It not only tells you if a buck is within range, but it also gives you the confidence to make the shot.

MH: That brings us to rifles, loads and shooting. Can you give us a few tips?

RM: To my mind a good antelope rifle shoots a 100- to 150-grain bul-let relatively fast and flat. The .243, .25/06 and .270 are good choices; the .30/06 would be the upper end. I recommend sighting-in 1½ inches high at 100 yards—and know exactly what your bullet is doing out at 300 and 400 yards.

The first shot at a standing antelope is important. Take your time and make it count. Having a bipod on your rifle helps. If you miss with the first shot, you're apt to get running shots after that, and things can get tough in a hurry.

MH: Let's wrap up by discussing a couple of your best pronghorn hunting strategies.

RM: Most people try to hide in cuts and coulees and behind ridges when they stalk antelope. That can work, but here's the problem with that approach: A buck sees you coming one minute and then you drop out of sight the next. These cat-and-mouse games can go on for a while, and the buck may eventually get nervous and spook. And if he spooks, he might kick it into high gear and run . . . for miles.

I go about it differently. After spotting a buck that I reckon is worth stalking, I walk slowly toward him, generally angling off to one side. I don't try to hide; I walk out in the open. The buck runs off, usually several times. He stops, looks back and sees me coming along methodically. Soon he loses his edge and doesn't sense danger. He might even get curious, stop and move slightly toward me. It may take two or three hours, but you can often work your way into shooting range like that. The tactic works best on lightly hunted ranches where bucks aren't too spooky.

Something else often works for me during the September rut. A dominant buck frequently leaves his does to confront smaller bucks. Sometimes he'll run them way off over the plains, but eventually he'll come back. Watch for this behavior, and when the buck is away from the herd, slip within shooting range of the does without blowing them out of the country. Sit tight and glass. When that herd buck circles back, take him.

Outdoor Life, August 1999

Odyssey for a World Record

BY LYLE WILLMARTH AS TOLD TO LEE KLINE

For Lyle Willmarth, hunting Colorado mountain goats was a 14-year quest rife with frustration. But in the end, Willmarth was ready, and the hunt was worth the wait.

Swinging around the rock outcrop crowding the turn in the road, it felt like I'd slammed into a wall. No matter how hard I pushed on the pedals, my mountain bike just hung there, suspended by the steep grade and fierce wind. Making an undignified dismount, I pushed the bike off the road behind the shelter of a boulder and took a breather. I still had five more miles of uphill travel to my campsite.

Sitting behind the rock, my thoughts shifted back to the circumstances that had led me to being here in the first place.

One spring day in 1972, Elmer Luce, a good friend who I grew up with in Holcomb, Wisconsin, had asked, "How'd you like to try bowhunting elk in Colorado this fall?"

Even as I said, "You bet!" I didn't know where the money would come from. Wisconsin only had whitetails and black bears to hunt, so the chance to see the mountains and bowhunt elk more than outweighed the minor funding inconvenience.

My tax refund check saved the day, Elmer and I went on that hunt, and although I returned to Wisconsin afterward, I never really left Colorado. It wasn't long before everything I owned was in my car, and I was Colorado-bound once again—this time for good. I had absolutely no idea what I'd do when I got there—besides bowhunt as much as possible. Eventually I moved to Hot Sulphur Springs, a small mountain town.

I spent the first couple of weeks in the state exploring the mountains. One of these forays took me up the highest paved road on the continent to the top of Mt. Evans, a 14,258-foot snow-covered peak that dominates the horizon west of Denver. A Colorado Division of Wildlife officer had told me that there were mountain goats in that area, and I wanted to see if I could find them.

In a day's hiking at 12,000 to 14,000 feet, I'd seen several goats and was totally fascinated by the creatures and the terrain they lived in. I knew right then I had to try hunting goats with my bow. What I didn't know was that it would take 11 years before I got MY first chance.

Colorado offers limited licenses for mountain goat hunting in eight specific units. Six of the units are considered firearms areas where hunters may use their choice of legal hunting arms—bow and arrow, muzzleloader or centerfire rifle. The other two units are open to bowhunting only. All licenses are issued by a random computer drawing, and each year the number of applicants far exceeds the available permits.

Year after year, I applied for the Mt. Evans hunting unit, and each time I received a rejection slip and the hollow feeling of having to wait until next year. But just before the application deadline for the 1985 license drawing, my bowhunting partner, Kurt Keskimaki, suggested, "Let's change things this year and apply for tags in the roughest area there is to hunt. Maybe we'll get lucky."

Now, goat country anywhere is some of the most rugged terrain on the continent. Some places are nastier than others, one being the San Juan Wilderness of Southwestern Colorado. Neither Kurt nor I were surprised when our bowhunting goat licenses arrived in the mail a few weeks after applying.

The day before the September 7 opening found us boarding a narrow-gauge train for a ride down the Animas River Canyon to a pre-selected drop-off point. Five hours of hard backpacking put us at

11,000 feet, on an incredibly rugged mountain range in the heart of the goat area.

We hunted hard for the first two days, but the only white we saw was snow. On the third day, just as the weather promised to break, down came a steady rain. Three days later the rain turned back to snow, and we were forced to spend the next 36 hours in our one-man backpack tents. I must have read the labels on my freeze-dried food packages at least a thousand times during those long hours.

When the weather finally broke enough so we could see, we had one day left to hunt. The last morning dawned crystal clear as Kurt and I left camp to hunt another basin to the north. Finding a white goat in all that snow seemed nearly impossible, and we alternately hiked and glassed for most of the morning. Finally, we spotted a lone goat bedded on a thin rock shelf near the top of a cliff.

Kurt had taken a fine billy a few years earlier in another area, and because I'd never had a chance at a goat, he generously insisted that I go after this one solo. He would stay in the basin to keep an eye on the animal and provide me with hand-signal directions.

I hadn't gone more than a few yards when it struck me that the traditional camouflage I was wearing just wasn't going to work. In all that snow, I must have looked like a cricket on a white sheet. The only thing I could think to do was hunt in my white silk long underwear. So, off came my clothes, and I began the stalk of a life-time in my long johns.

The bright sun kept me comfortably warm, but it was posing another problem. I had left my sunglasses in camp, and the sun's brilliance reflecting off the fresh snow gave me a killer headache. Within an hour, I was having trouble seeing even large contour changes on the steep mountainside and walking became treacherous.

Even though I glassed for several more hours, I never could find the goat again. As I made my way back to where Kurt waited, my head was pounding. After 11 years of waiting for a goat license, it looked like I'd have to "wait until next year" again.

The next morning we packed out to the narrow-gauge tracks for the trip home from a miserable, disappointing hunt. While waiting for the train, I made a solemn vow: Even if it took another 11 years, I'd be ready when I drew another goat permit and things would end up differently.

Three years later, I got the chance to test that vow, and things did turn out very differently indeed—in a way I could never have dreamed possible.

Unlike previous years, the Colorado Division of Wildlife had changed the 1988 season structure in the Mt. Evans unit by splitting it into two time periods with 10 licenses allotted for each hunt. This unit had always been the one I wanted to hunt but I could never draw the license for it. Although the area was a firearms unit, I intended to bowhunt.

When filling out my 1988 goat application I reasoned that the later hunt, which opened on September 19, might be less appealing to most hunters. The only road into the area traditionally closes to motor vehicles immediately after Labor Day, limiting access to a seven- to 14-mile hump on foot. A Canadian caribou hunt I had booked would also conflict with the timing of the first hunt, so the second season looked like my best possibility to draw a tag.

Whether my reasoning was on target or not, that's the way it worked out. Finally, my name was on a permit in the area I had wanted to hunt for 14 years.

I had scouted the area every year in anticipation of getting a license, only to end up making other hunting plans after the computer spit out the drawing results. Over the years, I had located several fine trophy-class goats, but with a permit in my pocket, my scouting trips intensified.

Throughout the summer, I made several trips into the area, always entering from a new direction. I was intent on finding as many good billies as possible. If I settled on one animal, there was a chance that one of the other 19 hunters might also find him and get there first. Having a couple of alternate choices seemed like the way to increase my odds of success.

A few days before leaving on the caribou hunt, I decided to make one more trip into the goat area. The hours of scouting had already paid off with the locations of several fine billies, but I wanted to take a look at a distant ridge I had never been on.

Just before daybreak, I parked my truck at a little turnout on the highway and started the four-mile hike to the ridge. As the sun rose, I alternately walked and glassed. About midmorning I spotted a single goat lying on a rocky shelf near the very top of the ridge. Even at 400 yards through my 10X25 binoculars, there was little question that this mountain goat was something special. As I cut the distance to around 100 yards, the goat spotted me and stood up.

Two other big billies I hadn't seen also got to their feet to eyeball me. With the other two goats providing perspective, it was immediately apparent just how special the first goat was. "Those horns have got to be more than 11 inches long," I thought to myself, but chalked the idea up to wishful thinking or goat fever. Eleven-inch horns on a mountain goat are virtually unheard of.

The standoff lasted several minutes before the goats decided I wasn't a threat and began feeding along the ridge above me. I decided to stalk closer to get a photo.

Slowly moving into some rocks along their path, I just lay there until the billies fed into range of my 200mm lens. At 20 yards, I snapped the last frame on the roll of film and quietly slipped out of sight.

Hiking back to the truck, all I could think of was the incredible size of the goat and the worrisome prospect of someone else finding him before I got back to the mountain. Reminding myself that most of the other hunters wouldn't get that far from the road, I headed for home to get ready for my Canada trip. On the way, I dropped the film off for processing.

Rested now, I pushed the loaded bicycle back onto the road and began pedaling again. Just hours earlier, I had returned from a very successful caribou hunt. Kissing my wife, Linda, hello and goodbye at the same time, I started loading my truck for the goat hunt. The season had opened earlier in the day, and remembering the road closure, I tossed in my mountain bike at the last second.

Bucking 20 to 30 mph head winds for another five miles, I pedaled to the same pullout I'd used during my last scouting trip. Darkness had long since settled over the mountain as I quickly pitched a spartan camp and tried to eat supper. Totally exhausted from the grueling ride, I didn't make it through the meal before sleep overtook me.

After a very short night, daybreak and nausea pried me out of the sleeping bag. The previous day's exertion and traveling from only 200 feet above sea level to more than 13,000 in less than 48 hours surely had something to do with my ills, but this was no time to be sick. I dressed, shouldered the pack and slowly started out along the ridge to where I'd last seen the big billy more than three weeks earlier.

Stiff winds hounded me as I hiked and glassed with no results. The morning hours slid by, and the growing fear that someone else might have already found the goat started to dominate my thoughts. I decided to cross the ridgeline for a last look at the facing mountain before making an early return to camp. Moments after crossing the ridge, my binoculars revealed three white specks feeding along the rocky slope about a mile away. All three billies were still there after all. The sun lit them up like beacons as they crested the mountaintop and disappeared from sight. I instantly forgot about being sick, and the wind no longer bothered me. A well-used goat trail circled the basin in that direction, and I quickly made my way to the spot on the ridge where the goats had gone out of sight.

The top of the ridge formed a large rounded knob before abruptly falling away to the south. Staying below the skyline and behind some large boulders, I slowly began to scan the mountaintop with my binoculars. About five seconds later, I found the goats right in the middle of the knob barely 100 yards away.

Dropping my pack where I sat, I nocked an arrow. Hugging the ground and staying behind rocks, I closed the distance inches at a time until just 20 yards separated me from the nearest goat.

Years of instinctive shooting practice took over and brought the 70-pound recurve into action. The arrow flashed across the alpine and disappeared just behind the foreleg of the largest billy. All three goats broke for the south, but at 50 yards one of them went down.

Slumping back against the nearest boulder, I sat for several min-utes—how long, I'm not sure—just soaking in every particle of the past few moments. It all seemed too good to be true.

Two hours later, the skinning and deboning of the meat finished, I still seemed to doubt my good fortune. Then I tried to pick up my pack. Believe me, the five miles back to camp convinced me that it all was for real.

In camp, I managed to get everything into my pack or tied on the mountain bike. Thank goodness it was all downhill to the truck. I coasted the entire 14 miles.

Total exhaustion had replaced all excitement as I arrived home late that night. I still didn't know just how good my goat was, and it didn't really seem to matter right then. My wife, Linda, had to help me get the pack in the house, and upon seeing the horns, she put a tape on

WILLMARTH'S MOUNTAIN BIKE proved valuable, although he had to stop frequently to let his brakes cool during the 14-mile trip down the mountain.

them. When the horn tips went past the 11-inch mark, I knew the goat was much better than I'd ever dreamed. I had forgotten about the photos from the scouting trip, but Linda had picked them up while I was in Canada. One of the pictures turned out to be an excellent closeup of a very large goat. When we studied it on a slide screen, there was little doubt it was of the same billy I had killed.

With a final score of 52⁴⁄₈, the goat was officially recognized as the new Pope and Young Club World Record at the bowhunting club's 1989 banquet. The score was also good enough to place the billy well up in the Boone and Crockett Club records and set a new state record for the species.

The life-size mount of that Colorado mountain goat now occupies my trophy room wall. Several plaques and the enlargement of my photo surround it. When I reflect on the years spent trying to draw a permit and the one miserably unsuccessful hunt, all I can say is, "It was well worth the wait!"

Outdoor Life, March 1992

Arctic Blast

BY JIM ZUMBO

Things are certainly different near the top of the world. But not so much that hunting won't make you a few pretty good friends.

s our boat slides through heaving swells pelted with frigid rain, I have to remind myself that I'm living a dream I've held for years: hunting musk ox in the Northwest Territories, 200 miles north of the Arctic Circle. My glasses and binoculars are so streaked I can hardly make out the point where sea ends and land begins. The nearest firewood is 600 miles to the south, at treeline.

"Musk ox!" my guide, George Angohiatok, suddenly exclaims, as if on cue. I wipe my glasses for the hundredth time and strain to see. Out on the misty tundra I finally spot several dark shapes moving slowly, but they're too far away to determine gender or size.

George and I beach the johnboat and join Mike—another of the week's five hunters—and his guide, David. Mike and I flip a coin to see who gets the first shot. He wins; I wince. We head out.

Although the wind is so much a presence you might think to hide behind it, the tundra is completely devoid of contour or cover and

MUSK OX often form a defensive line to intimidate predators.

we are in the middle of it. You can't get much more exposed than this. All we can do is advance slowly, hoping the animals will let us move close enough for a shot. The technique is by no means a hopeless one: Musk ox have no upright predators, so a stealthy walk is actually preferable to crawling—a crawling man is likely to be mistaken for a wolf, the animals' primary enemy. As we go, one of the musk ox rounds up the others, keeping them in a tight group. George tells us it's the herd bull.

When the musk ox continue to move away from us, George and David decide it's foolish to keep going and we head back to the boats to make our way up the Ellice River, toward which the oxen

are headed. The boats are 16-footers with 35- and 50-horse outboards that have the look of hard use. In the middle of the four-mile trip the rain turns to sleet. With every gust my wool clothes are uncovered by the useless poncho I'm wearing. It's amazing to me that the Inuits are able to survive here season after season. And this is still the last month of summer.

When George and David finally guide the boats to the shore, we climb up over the bank to see the herd feeding 500 yards away. It takes the two Inuits only a moment to pick out the herd bull again. Because a direct approach puts the animals on edge, Mike and David ease forward at an angle to the herd. Each time the animals assume a lumbering tack away from them, Mike and David patiently readjust their course and close distance. After 45 minutes, Mike's first shot blisters through the 50-mph wind and finds its mark. When the animal only lurches forward without falling, a second bullet has the fat lady singing.

As Mike and I approach the 700-pound bull with George, our eyes are as wide as schoolboys'. But our curiosity is cut short by a stroke of fresh luck.

"Another bull!" George says with his binoculars against his eyes. "Half a mile away and moving toward us."

At Mike's shot, the herd had run off over a rise in the tundra. Now another bull is feeding slowly in our direction 100 yards from the river. The sleet has let up a bit, replaced by a quiet snowfall: At last I can see more clearly. George and I ease along, moving slowly and using the riverbank as cover.

Half an hour later, we are only 150 yards from the bull. I carefully set up my shooting sticks, rest the 7 mm Mag rifle securely and take a deep breath of freezing air. Like Mike's, my first shot strikes the bull a killing blow, but instead of falling, the animal remains on his feet. I quickly chamber another round, set the crosshairs on his woolly shoulder and squeeze off the coup de grace.

As we ease up on him I marvel at the long hair and patches of wool—quiviut—on his pelt. The horns are long and thick at their bases. George believes the animal will make the record book, but that's not important. What's important is being in the Arctic and sharing the hunting experience with the Inuits, a people whose hardiness and warmth amaze me. Together, George and I dress, skin and quarter my animal. After hauling much of the meat to the boats, George offers a welcome suggestion: going back to camp, changing clothes and returning after we've gotten warm and dry.

The camp is shared by several Inuit families. They come from the village of Cambridge Bay on Victoria Island every August and September to catch char and hunt caribou. Dried fish hang outside the tents, and caribou quarters are piled on the rocks. One family has a commercial fishing license and gillnets 1,000 pounds of char a day. For the rest of the Inuits, though, the char that they spear and handnet in these two months are strictly for personal consumption over the long winter. Back in Cambridge Bay, many of the Inuits work at a DEW radar installation. Others sell handicrafts or trap through the winter.

The next day George invites me to fish with his family. We pile into the boat and head for a set of rapids six miles upstream where the char gather before ascending the falls. George and his sons, J.R., Ron and Brian, go to work catching fish. The char are stacked so thickly in the silty water that the men actually feel for their bodies with the nets and spears. Family members sit on rocks talking and eating raw fish livers and eggs, both coveted delicacies.

When more than a dozen char have been collected, J.R. builds a campfire in the rocks with willow twigs he's found scattered along the riverbank; the biggest are only as thick as a pencil. Butter quickly melts in a pan and soon the minutes-old char fillets are added. Twigs must be fed to the fire continually, but the effort is worth it: I can't remember having eaten more delicious fish. On our way downriver, we meet up with two other Inuit families from the camp and tie our boat to theirs. They've killed two caribou and are drifting down-stream celebrating their good fortune with cups of hot tea.

But even the Arctic cannot resist progress. "In the old days, we all used dogsleds to get around in the winter," George tells me. "Now we drive snowmobiles. Would you believe that we even use GPS to find our way?"

I think about that statement a lot, but it's comforting to know that some of the traditions are still intact, if only by the will of nature. As I board the plane, Mabel tells me to send some sun back to her. A snowstorm is coming.

Outdoor Life, January 1997

The Big Sheep

BY JIM ZUMBO

When they all look spectacular,
it takes a legendary guide—
and a lot of restraint—
to wind up with a "keeper."

W hen I showed up in the Flathead River drainage in northwest Montana in September of 1995, the first thing my guide did was lie to me. "The toughest part of this hunt was drawing the tag," said Jack Atcheson Jr. "Now it's a matter of lots of glassing and locating the ram we want."

Sure, Jack.

Don't get me wrong—I had no doubts about Jack's ability to find sheep. He's a longtime friend and quite possibly the finest sheep hunter in the world. But now I was finding out the true meaning of the phrase "unforgiving landscape." I'd been applying for this sheep tag for 15 years, and while I was waiting that had seemed like a long time. But as I groped my way across the brutally steep, boulder-strewn hillside—with rocks the size of Hyundais falling away beneath my feet—I began to ask myself, "What was the hurry?"

When I was nine years old, I was into toy dump trucks, Little League and merit badges. Not Atcheson. He was hunting sheep. Not to be confused with his father, Jack Atcheson Sr. (a legend in his own right whom I've hunted with as well), Jack Jr. completed the revered Grand Slam—taking all four North American subspecies—while still in his early 20s. And he recently discovered the remains of the biggest ram ever recorded

127

A LUCKY GUESS?

"THE RAM PICTURED ABOVE WAS TAKEN IN SOUTHEASTERN WASHINGTON, AND WAS THE FIRST PERMIT TO BE AUCTIONED OFF IN WASHINGTON STATE. TOM PAWLACYK (HOLDING THE RAM) PURCHASED THE PERMIT FOR $100,000, AND I (KNEELING NEXT TO TOM) GUIDED HIM. THIS RAM WAS 42 INCHES IN LENGTH AND VERY HEAVY-HORNED. TO MY KNOWLEDGE, IT IS THE LARGEST BIGHORN RAM KILLED BY A NONRESIDENT IN THE STATE OF WASHINGTON.

"I had a long time to watch this ram, and with a sharp stick I lightly scratched the measurement on the back of my hand so Tom had an idea of its estimated score. I felt it would score 187 points. When we measured it three days later, it scored exactly 187. I believe I got lucky, to be honest. Sixty days later it officially scored 185 4/8."

—Jack Atcheson Jr.

in the Lower 48. Now in his forties, the six-foot-tall Butte native has been a sheep guide for over 25 years. When some high-bidding hunter buys his way to a Governor's tag, Jack is a good bet to get the call.

To the uninitiated, all of Montana's rams look spectacular, and part of Jack's expertise is knowing the difference between a big ram and a really big one. I'd hunted and photographed sheep before, but this unit in the Flathead was special—it was primarily public land, and a good dozen of the rams here would easily make the Boone and Crockett record book. Jack said he'd seen one just a month before that could qualify as the all-time record. In other words, picking my shot would be a real challenge. Of course, just because you see a ram doesn't mean you can get at it—you can see Venus, too.

"The horns of a huge ram have a boxy look to them," Atcheson said, as he explained what makes the difference between a keeper and all the rest. "They're almost square. And if they drop down below the jaw, with plenty of mass all the way around, you know you're look-ing at an exceptional sheep." But I knew there was another factor in the equation, one Jack couldn't really describe. It's called experience. He just knows an exceptional animal when he sees one.

Living Large

Well, they all looked pretty good to me here on the "easy" part of the hunt—hanging off a 45-degree slope, dodging boulders and chasing animals much better adapted to both feats than I am. We moved into a recently burned forest, hiking along a ridge and stopping at rocky overlooks to glass the surrounding hillsides. We saw several rams feeding, but only one held Jack's interest.

The ram grazed across a canyon—a loner with what looked to be very thick horns close to a full curl. (Contrary to popular belief, genetics don't appear to be the deciding factor in producing large horns. Research conducted at Colorado State University suggests that the primary determinant is nutrition, followed by the animal's age and then its genes. More than anything else, the quality of Montana's for-age seems to account for its tremendous sheep.) We studied the lone ram for half an hour, then climbed to another position for a better look. He was in a hidden pocket, invisible except from where we'd first spotted him. If he hadn't been hidden so well, another hunter probably would have seen him already—and there was no doubt that any mere mortal would have gone after this ram immediately. But I was beyond that; I was with Jack.

"Let's leave him be for a day or two," Atcheson decided. "He's got plenty of length, but his bases don't seem to be very massive. I think we can do better."

I thought about my friends back home in Cody, Wyo. They'd never believe I was passing up this ram. And that wasn't all: That afternoon we came across six more, at least three of them record-book contenders. Again, Atcheson gave the thumbs-down, grinning as he watched me go into shock.

A Pair of Kings

The next morning, when it was barely light enough to see, Jack and I were back on the trail with the spotting scope. Soon enough he'd pinpointed a pair of rams, more than a mile and a half off.

"The big ram is a boomer," said my tutor. "He might be just what we're looking for. And the little one will easily make the book."

"How does the big one look for score?"

"He'll go 190, but we need to move in closer for a better look." 190. A magic number in sheep hunting. In Wyoming you'd stir-fry your own children to kill a 190 ram. But there was no rushing Jack. He figured it would take nearly half a day to get within shooting range of this pair, at which point we'd know if they were as worthy as they seemed from afar.

With the sun just coming up over the horizon, we headed around the rim to a point where we could drop down on the sheep. Working along the ridge wasn't tough, but I wasn't looking forward to the inevitable descent.

It was worse than I thought. I eased my way down, trying to keep noise to a minimum, but rocks clattered off at almost every step. Worse, the wind changed to the sheeps' advantage—assuming they were still in the area at all. We tried circling around to get downwind, but it was no use: The slope was even steeper, and we would have needed ropes to lower ourselves. We sat down to wait for the wind to shift.

It took half an hour to get the break we needed. Immediately, we continued our descent, looking now for the rams. In my mind's eye I had the scenario figured: Jack would find them, set up his spotting scope and evaluate the larger of the two. If he gave me the green light, I'd case into a prone position, find a solid rest and take my best shot.

THE DAMAGE

THE FIRST THING TO REALIZE ABOUT SHEEP HUNTING IS THAT ODDS ARE IT'S GOING TO HURT YOU—AND I'M NOT TALKING ABOUT YOUR BODY.

Unless you're a resident in a sheep state and are willing to hunt on your own, you're in for some hefty fees. But hunting alone isn't even an option much of the time: In Alaska and Canada, for example, all nonresidents must be guided. And most sheep country is so remote that anyone unfamiliar with the area is probably better off with a guide anyway. According to Jack Atcheson Jr. (406-782-3498), average prices for outfitted hunts for Grand Slam species run as follows:

- **Rocky Mountain bighorns** in the Lower 48: $7,000 to $9,000; in Canada: $15,000 to $19,000.

- **Desert bighorns** in the Lower 48: $8,000 to $10,000; in Mexico: up to $50,000.

- **Dall sheep** in Alaska: around $9,000.

- **Stone's sheep** in Canada: around $16,000.

But all of this assumes you've got yourself a tag. Big assumption. Almost all sheep tags in the Lower 48 are made available through a lottery or auction. The odds of drawing a tag depend on the popularity and success rate in a given unit. The odds of my drawing my Montana tag, for example, were about 1 in 100. Many states will provide statistics on the likelihood of drawing; some states give that data away, some make you pay for it. Many states—Wyoming, for one—now award preference or bonus points if you do not draw a tag, giving preference to your application as points accumulate from one year to the next. Governor's tags are usually auctioned to the highest bidder by the Foundation for North American Wild Sheep, with proceeds going back to the states for sheep management. Tags have sold for as much as $300,000.

Most states have a mandatory waiting period between a successful draw and your next application for a tag: In Wyoming, it's five years; in Montana, seven; in Colorado and Utah, you get one tag in a lifetime. See what I mean about that guide?

The Double Clutch

It didn't work out that way. Instead, the rams bolted from their beds and ran into a group of trees, where they stopped for a moment. They'd probably heard us without actually seeing us, and were doing a little spotting of their own.

The next thing I knew, Jack was shouting, "Shoot! Shoot!"

But I couldn't. The smaller ram was standing alongside the giant sheep, but on the far side. I couldn't risk the bullet penetrating the big ram and striking the smaller one. Then both of them broke and ran across the rocks, still abreast. I held my fire. My opportunity finally came when the big ram gained a full body length on his pal. They were just about to crest a ridgetop when I fired.

It was over. Jack got to the ram first, and you might say he was excited. Of course, so was I. The sheep had massive horns, but Jack was most impressed with the bases, which measured a whopping 17 inches. To put that into perspective, the world-record bighorn, taken in 1911, had only 16⅝-inch bases. Of the top 100 bighorns in the book, only three had 17-inch bases.

The ram's official score was 187, three inches shy of Jack's split-second call of 190. Which isn't very important except in one respect: It shows just how well Jack Atcheson Jr. knows sheep. Especially when you consider that a huge gouge in the measuring area of each horn dropped my total score by . . . three inches.

"How'd you judge that sheep's score right on the button in less than a second?" I asked.

"Dunno," Jack replied. "Guess I just felt it. There was never a doubt in my mind."

If I started now and spent every fall for the next 30 years with a spotting scope stuck in my eye, I might be able to pull that off, too; then again, those rocks would be looking extra large by then. No, when you come right down to it, there's no substitute for getting your experience early. And in Jack's case, he got a hell of a lot of it.

Outdoor Life, May 1996

DANGEROUS
GAME

Days of Swine . . . and Noses

BY BOB McNALLY

Wild hogs are hairy, smelly, ill-tempered, and loud. The trick is not in stalking them—it's in keeping your nerve.

I heard the hogs long before I saw them. The loud squealing and deep grunting put me on full alert in the darkened end of the swamp in which I'd been stalking.

The black, muck-covered South Carolina creek bottom was loaded with sign from rooting hogs. Huge, random chunks of ground had been upturned as if by a plow gone berserk. No green leaves, no mushrooms, no acorns or hickory nuts, no grass, not a single shoot remained on the ground. Fresh tracks were scattered everywhere in the moist soil. Tree trunks were caked with dried mud two feet off the ground, an indication that large pigs had scratched and rubbed their muddy bodies against the bark.

At dawn that day I'd positioned myself in a tree stand from which I could watch two game trails near the creek and a well-used hog wallow, all within shooting distance. A sow and its piglets had come to indulge in the mud, but like a doe with fawns, such game isn't fair shooting, and I held off.

No boars showed themselves, so at midmorning I climbed down and stillhunted into the wind along the creek. In bowhunting, stalking often turns out to be more like scouting than actual hunting. But with wild hogs the method can be extremely productive. A pack of wild hogs is about as subtle as a rototiller. They are ill-mannered beasts that constantly fight over food. And they regularly feel the urge to pronounce dominance. When they battle for the favor of sows it can sound as if the gates of hell have been cast open.

I was several hundred yards from my stand, still working along the creek, when bellowing and squealing broke the silence. I leaned against a cypress for cover and scanned ahead with binoculars, picking my way through the underbrush, trying to make out a flank or catch the slightest movement. I waited 10 minutes, hoping the hogs would work my way, but it was obvious from the raucous squalling that they were holding in one place. I planned my stalk.

The soft soil was made for silent walking, and there were plenty of mature oaks for camouflage. I slipped from tree to tree, covering about 100 yards, working into the breeze. Then I caught the scent of swine hanging in the humid air. There's nothing quite like it. It's not a particularly offensive odor; it's just different—a pungent, musty aroma of mire, ooze, and muck combined with a distinct animal smell. Once you get a snootful, you never forget it.

As I gathered the scent, I went on point, knowing the hogs had to be close. I nocked an arrow, leaned against a big water oak, and scanned the brush ahead. The pigs had to be close, but I didn't locate exactly where before a squeal behind me brought the hair up on my neck. I spun around, arrow at the ready. As my eyes searched the foliage behind me, squeals, grunts, and popping hog jaws seemed to come from several directions. Then, 15 yards away, I saw a flash of running hog moving from right to left. It was a 100-pound sow, bawling and groaning as it went. And right behind the sow was an even bigger and madder boar.

The sow was in season and the boar knew it, but apparently they were having a lovers' quarrel. A loud lovers' quarrel. The sow bolted through the timber but turned near my tree, heading back upwind. Shooting at running game with a bow isn't something I usually recommend, but the boar was close and right on the sow's tail. So I picked a spot between two big oaks 20 yards away where the sow would have to pass, and I came to full draw. When the boar's nose touched the opening, I released my arrow. I never saw the shaft in flight, but it hit with the crack of a Cal Ripken line drive, and the boar came to a mud-flying, hoof-skidding, body-shaking halt.

My arrow was buried to the feathers behind its shoulder. But it just turned and looked right at me. Figuring I'd caused the loss of its girlfriend and had something to do with 30 inches of carbon shaft through its chest, the boar did exactly what you would expect. It dropped its head and came flat out at me on a straight-line charge.

Right then I realized I had made the ultimate hog-hunting error: I did not have an escape plan in place when my arrow was loosed.

There was nowhere to go. No fallen timber to jump. No trees with low branches to climb. Nowhere to hide from the oncoming, razor-edged tusks driven by 200 pounds of hairy ham.

I was screwed. I now know what Wile E. Coyote feels like in a Road Runner cartoon. Standing still and holding an arrowless bow, I looked left, then right, then up for an escape route, but none was to be had. Then I turned to check on the hog, which was bearing down like the space shuttle gone haywire—and looking just as big.

One second before impact of hog and human, I jumped sideways behind the oak I'd used for cover. The pig went thundering by, hooves flailing, splattering mud and swamp ooze. For a moment I thought perhaps the hog hadn't really charged me. Maybe I was only in its escape path. That's when it turned with such fury and put on the brakes so hard it crashed. But as quickly as it fell, it leaped back onto its feet and lined me up again.

When it faced me, so help me, that pig's facial expression changed. It stood there at 20 yards and looked straight at me as if to say, "Okay, Arrow Boy, maybe I'm a goner, but you're going down too." With that, it ducked its head and charged harder than the first time.

Going into rodeo-clown mode again, I jumped behind the tree to dodge the hog's rush. As it went hurtling past it slashed at me with its tusks, missed, then crumpled to its knees, sliding and falling dead at last.

That wasn't the first time I've been charged by an arrow-hit wild hog, but it sure was the most memorable. And that's precisely why bowhunting feral pigs is so much fun and why it's becoming one of the most popular big-game pursuits in the country. Wild pig hunting is in such high demand that pay-to-hunt ranches are springing up in many states, particularly in the South. In California, the year-round season has become very popular. Some years the take of feral swine has actually been greater than the Golden State's deer harvest.

Hog hunting is permissible in nearly two dozen states, and public hunting land in hog country is abundant. The country's wild hog population, in most cases, consists of domestic stock gone wild. After several generations the animals degenerate from farm-fattened pink Porkys into hairy, narrow-hipped, long-tusked porkers. Because they're not considered native animals and not categorized as game animals in many areas (especially on state and federal property), they're seen as destructive pests that authorities want eliminated. Pigs also breed year-round, so they can quickly overpopulate an area, which is why hog limits and seasons are usually liberal, especially for bowhunters. Many states have no closed season. And because hogs can be ruinous to farm crops, permission to bowhunt private land is much easier to get than with deer, turkeys, and other game.

THE LONG, SHARP TUSKS of a wild hog are very dangerous to both man and dog.

Another plus if you want to bowhunt pigs is that no special equipment is needed if you're already a deer hunter. The same bows and arrows, camouflage, tree stands, and hunting skills used for deer work for hogs. However, pigs are tough, with thick hides and lots of fat. You'll need a wide-blade, razor-sharp broadhead to make a fair shot on a heavy hog.

It's also smart to plan an escape route in advance, just in case.

Outdoor Life, December 1995

SWINEALIA

✔ Wild hogs have roamed North America since Hernando de Soto brought them to Florida in 1539.

✔ Both male and female wild hogs have tusks, and the upper and lower tusks overlap. The constant gnashing of teeth serves to continually hone the tusks, making them formidable weapons.

✔ Javelinas (also called collared peccaries), which are native to the southwestern United States and Mexico, are not to be confused with wild hogs or Russian boars. In the U.S., both of the latter are feral, while javelinas, though related, are true wild (and much smaller) pigs.

✔ Contrary to popular opinion, no purebred so-called Russian or Prussian wild boars roam America's forests. Some mixed-breed Russian feral hogs exist in parts of Tennessee, Texas, and New Hampshire, but their European genes are diluted.

✔ Pigs don't sweat, so they can't take much heat or sun. They seek out cool, moist areas to maintain normal body temperature in hot weather.

✔ Wild hogs are gregarious animals that commonly live in family groups. However, large males often become solitary and can be extremely difficult to hunt.

✔ Huntable wild hog populations are found in the following states: Alabama, Arizona, Arkansas, California, Florida, Georgia, Hawaii, Kentucky, Louisiana, Mississippi, New Hampshire, New Mexico, North Carolina, Oklahoma, South Carolina, Tennessee, Texas, Virginia, and West Virginia.

✔ Wild hogs grow fast, attaining weights of 80 to 100 pounds in their first year. However, stories about 300- and 400-pound wild hogs are fantasy. Most mature feral pigs peak at about 150 pounds (live weight), and a 250-pounder is a monster.

✔ Some mature wild hogs have a tough, gristlelike plate behind each shoulder called a shield. On a large boar the shield can be nearly an inch thick and can deflect an arrow like armor. For this reason a bowhunter should try to take a quartering-away shot on a big boar, which allows an arrow to slip behind the shield and into the hog's chest cavity.

Death Came Running— Twice

BY TOM JESIOLOWSKI AS TOLD TO BRUCE BRADY

I've faced many charges from grizzlies and brown bears in my work as a guide and photographer, but almost all of them were bluffs in which the bear stopped or backed off. But on back-to-back hunts, the only way to stop the bear was with a rifle.

It was a big brown bear, and though it was more than a mile away, I could tell that it was in prime condition after a summer of feeding on spawning salmon. The bear was on the mountain across the valley and was moving up a well-worn bear trail toward high country. The pelt glistened and shook with each step, and it seemed to change color as the wind whipped through it. The bear was beautiful.

"Take a look at this, Chip," I said, moving away from my spotting scope.

Chip wormed into position and squinted through the eyepiece. For several seconds, he looked in silence. Then I heard him whisper, "I don't believe it." That he was impressed did not surprise me, for I have yet to meet the man who is unmoved by these great bears.

Norman "Chip" Gerry was up from Georgia for his first Alaska hunt, and he hoped to shoot a big brown bear and a caribou. It was my job to help him succeed. I am a guide, and I work with outfitter Richard Guthrie of Anchorage. Richard's hunting outfit is top-notch. We hunt the Alaska Peninsula for brown bears and caribou, and the North Slope of the Brooks Range for Dall sheep, moose, caribou, and barren-ground grizzlies.

I hail from Pennsylvania. But in the mid 1970s, I came to Alaska for a hunt, and I was so captivated by the land and its animals that I stayed. During the off-season, I work as a taxidermist and freelance photographer, and I run my own business, Northland Arts, in Anchorage.

When I looked again at the big bear plodding up toward the rim, I had to smile. It looked as though this was going to be a lucky hunt. Chip wanted a bear that would square out at about nine feet, and this one appeared to measure up. We were fortunate to locate it on the first day of the hunt. I wasn't worried when the bear disappeared over the rim because the stream in the valley still had a strong run of spawning salmon, and I was certain that our bear would be back.

Chip wanted to go after the animal, but I advised against it, knowing that we could not keep pace. We had to wait for its return. It might take an hour or even a week, but sooner or later I was sure the bear would come back. In the meantime, we would look for another bear.

Within a half-hour, the weather suddenly began to change, as it often does on the Peninsula. The temperature dropped, the wind started to howl, and a violent rainstorm began. We huddled together in our slickers, peeking out now and then to check the distant bear trail. We toughed it out for six hours until the fading light forced us to begin the four-mile hike back to camp.

It was good to get out of that driving rain when we reached camp. In a short time, we had hot coffee and a steaming supper on the table. Coffee and hot grub have a way of changing a man's mood.

The wind and rain pounded our shelter and drove moisture through even the most microscopic pores of the tent fabric. But we were warm and dry, and we talked about the bear we had seen. Chip was full of questions such as: How big? How much does it weigh? And then there were the "what if" questions that all inexperienced bear hunters ask.

The next morning, the storm continued to rage in off the sea. We tried to hunt for a while, but the visibility was too limited to make it worth the effort. Back in the tent, Chip asked about dangerous encounters that I'd had with bears, and that made me remember many things.

From the beginning of my life in Alaska, I was fascinated by the big bears. I am still bemused by the power and controlled fury I sense every time I am in their presence. I have made many trips to McKinley National Park, and I have spent countless hours with the grizzlies there. Many times, I have been closer to one of them than it was smart to be. I couldn't give Chip an accurate count on the number of times I have been charged, both in the park and in the wild, but I estimated it to be 25 to 30 times. In a few instances, I had to make a hasty retreat, but all of the charges were bluffs in which the bear either turned aside or pulled up short. A grizzly once harassed me for four days, but that is another story. The thing that a man in bear country can never forget is that a bear is totally unpredictable and always dangerous. You only have to witness a fight between two of them to know forever how fast, powerful, and utterly violent their fury can be.

The next morning, we were happy when the rain slacked off enough for us to hunt. While Chip got his gear together, I rustled up some bacon and eggs and slipped into my old, lucky jack-shirt. It's superstitious, perhaps, but I had worn it on several hunts when big bears were taken.

It was still early when we reached our hunting area. We forded the salmon stream and began climbing toward a rockslide 300 yards above us. The elevation would provide a clear view of the bear trail on the ridge to the west. We had only climbed a short distance when I spotted our bear moving down the same trail it had used on the first day.

If the bear continued on that course, it would descend into a large alder patch that bordered a narrow feeder creek in the valley below. I figured that the bear would work through the alders and then follow the tributary creek to its confluence with the salmon stream.

We hurried downhill, forded the river, and scrambled across a number of sloughs and ditches. Our plan was to take a downwind stand near the end of the alder patch and catch the bear cold when it emerged from the thicket.

We reached our stand and expected the bear at any second, but an hour later our bear had not appeared. It was my guess that it had bedded down in the alders, so we decided to move westward and climb partway up the ridge it had descended to see whether the increase in elevation would help us spot the animal in the brush.

We had been glassing for a half-hour when we spotted a second large bear a mile or so to the north. The big animal was moving through alders and coming directly toward us. Climbing a rocky outcropping 100 yards to the north would provide us with a perfect shot if the bear continued on course, so we scrambled toward the outcropping, crossing a deep ravine on the way. We lost sight of the bear for only a few minutes, but the bear somehow vanished.

After an hour of glassing to no avail, I decided to descend the ridge on the upwind side of the alder patch where the first bear had disappeared. I felt sure it was still in there, and I thought my scent might flush it into the open and give Chip a shot.

In a short time, the bear emerged and quartered northward into the wind. A moment later, Chip's big .375 Magnum roared, and the big brown went down. We watched for a while and then moved down to confirm the kill. Chip was delighted because it looked as though the bear would square out at around nine feet. There was a lot of back-slapping and yelling, as there always is when a hunter takes his first bear. I think the elation comes as much from the sudden relaxation of tension as from the success of the hunt.

Chip dug out his camera only to discover that the previous day's drenching had locked it up. He wanted to take pictures before I skinned the bear, so there was nothing to do except return to camp and get my camera. It would be an eight-mile hike, round trip, but if we hurried, there would still be enough daylight for pictures when we returned.

I took the lead, and we talked about Chip's forthcoming caribou hunt while we hiked. I told Chip that if our luck held and he got his bull as easily as he had gotten his bear, he would be able to enjoy some wonderful goose shooting during the remainder of his stay.

We crossed through the alders from which our bear had come and then paused at the creek bank to empty the chambers of our rifles because it would be a slippery crossing. I descended the bank, waded the creek, and climbed up the other side. I went on for several yards before stopping to watch for Chip's appearance. He was just coming into view when I heard the bear.

There was a loud wuff, and the bear snapped its jaws. I wheeled around and saw a large brown bear coming down on me. It was only 30 paces away. I knew instantly that this bear meant to kill me. There was something different about the bear's wuff. It seemed to come from deep in its gut. There was also the incredible acceleration of its charge. I hadn't seen that in any of the other charges I had faced.

The next few seconds are difficult to describe, but I know that time seemed to speed up and many thoughts raced through my head. I remember thinking how odd it was that those big silvery ears were standing up, rather than laid back as they usually are when a bear makes a rush. There was no fear in the strict sense of the word—only disbelief. I recall thinking, "This is really happening, and this bear is going to get me. "

My rifle hung by its sling from a hook on the side of my pack frame. I must have grabbed for it out of instinct, for I knew for sure that there was no time in which to chamber a round before the bear would be on me.

On the last stride, the bear's front legs cleared the ground, and the animal reached for me. As I turned away, I poked the barrel of my rifle in the bear's chest and pulled the trigger, knowing full well that the firing pin would fall on an empty chamber. It was a futile gesture, but it seemed to be the only thing left for me to do.

A split second before the collision, the bear's mouth gaped open and its head turned slightly to the side, as though the bear were making some final and deadly adjustment in the way it intended to strike. The power of the blow was incredible. It was like being hit by a runaway truck. Our motion was so violent that I was amazed that the bear could still be coordinated enough to gather me in with those massive forepaws. I felt no pain when claws raked across my forehead and cheek.

We crashed into the base of an alder clump five yards from the place where the bear's full weight had driven into me. There was this feeling of immense pressure, and I thought that my insides must surely be bursting.

I was lucky that I piled up on my side rather than on my back, because my pack frame took the brunt of the fury for the first moments. The bear's jaws were snapping like trip hammers, and it attacked in a wild rage. The speed and savageness of the assault reminded me of the way two dogs go at each other when they fight to kill. The motions were so quick that there was no way to even consider any kind of defense. There was a horrible feeling of total helplessness. And still I felt no pain and had no idea where the bear was tearing at me.

In the next moment, it was rooting beneath my pack frame as though trying to get at my neck. I knew that if the bear succeeded, it would be all over in an instant. "Kill him, Chip!" I screamed. "Kill him!" And then the thought flashed through my mind that I could be shot to death in the next second.

The jaws closed on my side, and the upper teeth dug into my back. Then I was whipped off the ground, and the bear was shaking me like a terrier shakes a rat.

Then I heard the .375 Magnum roar, and I dropped to the ground, my leg twisted under me. I could see the bear run away, and it was then I realized that I still had my Winchester in my hand. Somehow, the bolt had been thrown back, and in the next second I put a cartridge in the chamber, but the bear had vanished into the brush.

Chip ran up as I straightened my leg. "Get ready!" I screamed. "He'll come again. Be ready!" We waited in silence, our rifles raised.

I asked Chip if he were sure that he had hit the bear, and he told me he was sure that he had put a slug into the rump. He had deliberately fired at the bear's rump to make sure he would not hit me. The chance to do that had come when the bear lifted me off the ground and shook me. The bear had run away with a limping gait, which seemed to indicate that it was wounded.

It's strange, but for some time after the bear broke off his attack, the extent of my wounds did not enter my head. "This is fantastic," I remember thinking. "One bear dead, and a wounded one in the brush."

Chip helped me to my feet, and I began to wonder how much damage the bear had done to me. At that instant, there was snapping in the brush, and we saw the bear 50 feet away just as it began to run. I guess I acted on impulse because I sprinted after the animal. As the bear crossed an opening, I put it down with my .338 Magnum. I eased up and shot again to make sure that the bear was down for keeps.

Suddenly, the hairs on the back of my neck began to crawl with fear, and I also felt anger well up inside me. The bear had almost killed

me. We didn't even want to shoot the animal, and now it was dead. I walked up and yelled, "Dumb SOB!" and kicked the carcass as hard as I could. It was stupid, I know, but that's what I did.

Chip settled me down, and we removed my shirt to see how badly the bear had hurt me. There were seven or eight puncture wounds in my shoulder and the same number in my side below the armpit and in my back under the shoulder blade. A hole had been scooped out of my back. Then I began to feel pain and had muscle spasms over my ribs. I wondered about internal bleeding. Thankfully, there was no frothy blood coming out of my chest wounds. That would have indicated lung damage.

While Chip was giving me first aid, I thought about what had happened. The bear Chip killed wasn't the first bear we had seen but the second one. Despite all of the racket we had made over Chip's kill and all of the human scent flooding into the alders, the first bear had held tight and waited for a chance to get at us.

We still faced a four-mile hike to camp, and we both knew that if I went into shock, our problems would be insurmountable. Richard made regular afternoon flights over camp to check on us, and we had to get there before he flew over. If we missed him, it would be the following afternoon before I could get out and receive medical attention.

I was feeling the pain, especially in my ribs, but I knew I was lucky to be walking away from the attack. I knew, too, that if it had not been for Chip's cool head and good shooting, that raging bear would have finished me. It was a tough hike, but we made it to camp, and Chip immediately scratched the word "HELP" in the beach near our tent. He was just beginning to clean my wounds when Richard buzzed overhead and then landed.

We radioed the Cold Bay airport to have a medical team standing by and to divert a flight from Dutch Harbor to pick me up for the flight to Anchorage. By 7 p.m., I was in the hospital. The doctors shot me full of antibiotics, stitched up some of my wounds, and attached drain tubes to others. In addition to the wounds already mentioned, I had four broken ribs. Also, the ribs on my left side had been separated from the breastbone. Through it all, I never went into shock.

The morning after the attack, Richard and Chip returned to skin out Chip's bear, which was in good shape. But the bear that mauled me had been torn to pieces by other bears during the night. Both of the bears we killed turned out to be unusually large females.

During the next several months while I was healing, I had to do some soul searching about the coming spring bear hunt. Time has a way of healing psychological wounds as well as physical ones, and by the time the season rolled around, I was ready to go again. My wife, Mary Lou, talked against it, but I decided to go anyway. Maybe

I had to prove to myself that I could still deal with the big bears.

A short time later, my hunter, Willard Ryan from Mississippi, and I had just topped a ridge where we planned to glass the surrounding hills. I soon spotted a large bear in the valley far below, and I watched as it ambled toward the trail Willard and I had walked. I made no effort to move toward the bear because I was certain that as soon as it struck our scent, it would bolt out of the country.

What I saw next made my blood run cold. The bear reached our path and began to trail us up the slope. We watched in disbelief as the bear climbed the ridge below us, following our route step by step. The higher the bear climbed, the faster it moved. Once again, I had a mysterious knowledge that this bear was coming for us.

"Chamber a round, Willard," I said as calmly as I could. "I think we're going to have trouble with this bear."

We had enough elevation to see the bear when it made the top of the ridge some 300 yards away. The ridge crest rose and fell, so we saw the bear each time it topped a rise. The bear was still more than 100 yards away when it broke into a steady run.

"Get ready, Willard!" I urged. "He's coming for us!" There was a rise 30 yards away, which meant that we wouldn't be able to see the brown until it was almost on us.

An instant later, we heard brush breaking, and then the huge bear crashed into view, roaring and bearing down on us. We were standing about 10 feet apart, and we fired almost simultaneously. Both shots ripped into the bear's chest, and when it finally fell, I could have touched its nose with the muzzle of my rifle. We sat down and stared at the giant. My knees were weak, and I noticed that Willard's hands had begun to shake. The bear later squared out at more than 10 feet. It was a nerve-racking experience, one I'll always remember on future hunts. Man-scent had put the bear into a rage, or maybe it was the old lucky shirt; it seems to attract big bears. Whatever the cause, I am beginning to think that these big devils have it in for me.

The lesson learned is always the same. Bears are unpredictable, and they are always dangerous.

Outdoor Life, June 1986

Don't Bugle Up a Grizzly

BY BILL McRAE

Using an elk call in grizzly country may turn out to be a lot like bringing in a coyote with a varmint call. I did it, and let me tell you that facing a grizzly's charge with only a bow and arrow is not a calming experience.

Huge, wet snowflakes swirled like butterflies through the stovepipe opening in the tent roof and fell hissing on the hot stove. It was 4 a.m. on the kind of morning when one would rather crawl back into his sleeping bag than go hunting, but Skip Clark and I knew that if we didn't go out, we'd hate ourselves for the rest of the day. It's hell to have a conscience. We had come to the Bob Marshall Wilderness in Montana to bowhunt bugling bull elk, and no matter how deep the snow, we intended to hunt.

At the edge of a meadow on a small rise about two miles from camp, just at dawn, Skip bugled a couple of times, hoping that some lovesick bull would answer and betray his whereabouts. No answer came, and after a few minutes, we moved on.

It stopped snowing shortly after daybreak, but the white stuff was piled high on every branch, and it seemed to delight in avalanching down on us as we passed by. The elk wouldn't respond to bugling. They weren't moving either, and about 10 a.m., wet, tired, and disgusted, we decided to separate and head back to camp. Clark stillhunted through the timber, while I took the trail so as to get to camp ahead of him and start the fire and fix lunch.

Upon reaching the knoll where Clark had bugled the first time, I found something that raised the hair on the back of my neck. Leading directly to the spot where we had stood were the tracks of a medium-size grizzly bear. It had paused briefly, no doubt sniffing our tracks, and had then backtracked us for about 50 yards before moving on. As I studied the story in the snow, I wondered if the bugling had attracted the bear. It was a sobering thought.

Five days later, after the snow had melted and turned the trails to ribbons of mud, something similar happened. We had left camp long

before daylight to hunt several miles away. Things had frozen during the night, and a nearly full moon hung in the sky. Again, two miles from camp, but on a different trail, we stopped to bugle. After about five minutes, a deep-voiced bull answered from far below on the other side of the valley.

Clark exchanged insults with the bull again to confirm his location. "If we hurry, we can be there by daylight," he whispered. "Let's go!"

We hadn't gone 50 yards when Clark grabbed my shoulder and pointed at the ground. The puddles in the trail were covered with a thin layer of ice. There, illuminated by a shaft of moonlight, were the tracks of a very large grizzly, and water was still oozing back into them. We went on after the bull, although we did look over our shoulders more than usual.

It could have been coincidental that the bears showed up when and where they did. The Bob Marshall Wilderness is good grizzly country, and finding tracks is fairly common. During one of our hunts in the

same area the previous year, a grizzly took an elk quarter off a meat pole right next to our tent. But during the previously described hunt, the logical explanation is that the grizzlies were attracted by Clark's expert bugling. They were probably disappointed to find human beings instead of elk. If so, the implications are serious for anyone who, for whatever reasons, goes around imitating elk in grizzly country.

Why would grizzlies respond to an elk bugle? The reason, I think, is quite simple. Grizzlies are ravenous predators. They are ravenous, not because they're vicious, but because, as hibernators, they must crowd a whole year's worth of eating into about seven months. Consequently, they are attracted by any sight, sound, or smell that suggests food.

Back in my salad days as a wildlife photographer, I used to call grizzlies by imitating the sound of a rabbit in distress. It was insane, but it worked. If conditions were right, which wasn't always the case, the bears literally came running for an easy meal. Lest someone should try this stunt, I know of one photographer who did it in Alaska after taking the precaution of climbing a windfall first. The grizzly, a sow with cubs, charged, climbed the windfall, dragged the photographer down, and mauled him. The bear almost killed him. No photograph is worth the risk.

Sure, grizzlies eat rabbits, but do they prey on elk? Indeed they do! The only thing in question is the extent to which they do it. As I see it, there are three situations in which grizzlies utilize elk for food. The first is when an elk is carrion—the elk having died and its flesh having begun to decay.

Carrion is a major source of food, especially in the spring, and the bears can locate it at great distances with their supersensitive noses. They are also attracted by the ravens that congregate in noisy flocks around carcasses.

Grizzlies also prey on live elk in the spring. They take newborn calves and mature animals weakened by the ravages of winter. I saw a lot of evidence of the latter in the mid-1960s when I was photographing grizzlies in Wyoming's Yellowstone National Park.

For example, one day, while driving from Madison Junction to Old Faithful, I passed a large herd of elk in the Lower Geyser Basin. Two miles farther down the road, I saw a beautiful silvertip grizzly sow with three yearling cubs. The fearsome foursome was moving in the general direction of the elk. I should have put two and two together and followed them, but I figured the elk were safe from attack because they were on the other side of the Firehole River and out in the open. However, when I came back about an hour later, the elk were on the far side of the geyser basin, and they were running away. In the spot where they had been, at least 150 yards from the nearest tree, I saw the grizzlies. They had pulled down an elk and were feeding on it. I had missed witnessing the event and getting some great pictures by a matter of minutes.

I later talked to a park ranger who had actually witnessed a kill. He said it was a rather gruesome affair because the bears began to feed on the elk while it was still alive.

The third situation, and the one that we are most concerned about, is killing elk during the summer and fall, particularly during the rut. That's when the elk are healthy and the calves can run as fast as their mothers. The grizzly's effectiveness as a predator is really tested.

The question is whether the grizzly is mainly a scavenger that feeds on carrion, calves, and winter-weakened elk or a first-class predator capable of taking healthy elk and other large mammals at any time. Most of the older scientific texts reflect the first view, but in recent years, there appears to have been a change in thinking on the part of wildlife experts. Grizzlies are omnivorous, and they consume a lot of vegetation—broad-leaved herbs, roots, grasses and sedges, berries, pine nuts, and so forth. They also eat rodents, insects, and fish, but it is the grizzly's role as a meat-eating predator of large mammals that concerns us.

Studies conducted by the Interagency Grizzly Bear Study Team in Yellowstone National Park have shown that ungulates (hoofed mammals) constitute an important part of the grizzly's diet, and while deer, bison, and moose are eaten, the main meat source in the park is elk. A chart showing proportionate contributions of food sources to net digested energy indicates that the utilization of ungulates is highest in April, at over 70 percent. This drops to around 9 percent in August, and the percentage rises again through September and October to as high as 45 percent. September and October, of course, bring the rut.

Gary Brown, assistant chief ranger and head of the bear management program in Yellowstone National Park, said in an interview: "In the park in recent years, we've seen a great deal of predation by grizzly bears on elk, and I think that since the closure of the dumps, the bears are more and more learning to hunt and utilize the ungulate population."

On the possibility of attracting grizzlies by bugling, Brown said, "I think that a hunter has a good chance of attracting a bear, not only because of the association of the sound with the food source, but maybe because of curiosity. Grizzlies are very, very curious animals."

Another expert who regards grizzlies as first-rate predators is Keith Aune, a wildlife biologist for the Montana Department of Fish, Wildlife, and Parks. Aune has spent six years studying the bears on the East Front of the Rocky Mountains in Montana. His work involves attaching radio collars to bears and then monitoring, from an airplane and on the ground, the bears' activities. He is also a bowhunter.

Aune said, "Our radio data strongly indicates that some grizzlies in this area, particularly three or four large males, prey on elk on a regular basis. There is a lot of predation during the calving season, but we also find evidence of it on adult elk, both cows and bulls, throughout the summer and fall." Regarding the rut, Aune said, "There are certain bears that almost invariably hang around groups of elk, and they especially seem to zero in on areas where there is heavy rut activity."

I asked Aune if he thought a grizzly would attack a mature bull during the rut. He said, "From evidence I've seen at actual kill sites, it appears that they will take calves, big bulls, and everything in between."

Both Brown and Aune indicated that preying on elk was a learned behavior and that some bears are much better at it than others.

None of this means that grizzlies are a threat to elk populations. They certainly are not. My only point is that grizzlies do kill elk and, thus, anyone who tries to bugle up an elk in grizzly country should beware.

In the incidents described earlier with Skip Clark, we never actually saw the grizzlies involved, but we did see their very fresh tracks on top of our own. On another hunt, also in the Bob Marshall Wilderness, I got a look at a grizzly that I'll never forget.

My camp mates were Keith Aune and a retired game warden named Gene Sherman, but on a cold, rainy September 20, I hunted alone, as I often do. I was following a heavily used game trail about five miles from camp and was more or less lost—which isn't unusual for me. It was mid-morning, and figuring that the elk would be bedded for the day, I bugled every 100 yards or so, hoping that if I got close to a harem, the herd bull would feel threatened and answer. The trail snaked up a mountainside and finally into a pass where a mineral lick was located in a cathedral-like stand of huge lodgepole pines.

The lick was about 10 feet in diameter and situated on a slope. It was about one foot deep on the low side where the trail led past it, and it was three feet deep on the uphill side. There were deer and elk tracks in the lick. One thing puzzled me. A rock that weighed at least 100 pounds had been moved approximately 18 inches from where it had been embedded about halfway underground at the base of the lick's upper wall. It appeared that the rock had been moved recently, because although it had snowed and rained for three days, the edges of the cavity left by the rock were still quite crisp. I realized that pulling the large rock free and moving it required great strength and dexterity. Because a deer or an elk couldn't have done it, it must have been a bear, I concluded. I planned to ask Keith Aune if grizzlies used licks when I got back to camp.

I don't know how long I stood there pondering the mystery of the rock, but when I finally moved on, I found two indistinct trails that led in the direction I wanted to go. I started on the higher of the two, but when it petered out in a jungle of windfalls after about 50 yards, I turned around, went back to the lick, and took the lower trail.

After going about 30 yards, I decided it was worse than the first, so I headed back toward the lick to take the higher one again. Just as I started back, I heard huffing and crashing near the lick. Looking up, I saw what I took to be a black bear running toward me. I reached for an arrow because I had a black bear license, but in the same instant, I saw the bear's shoulder hump and broad head and realized that it was a huge dark-colored grizzly. My hand then went to my hip for my .44 Magnum revolver. The firearm was back in camp.

It all happened incredibly fast, but the images etched in my mind are of the grizzly coming, covering at least 20 feet at a bound, making a thumping noise and woofing each time it hit the ground, and I can still see the bear veering at the last instant to pass on my right, thank God. In the split second the bear was airborne as it bounded past me, the grizzly swung its massive head toward me. Its eyes met mine, but then the bear looked away to see where it would land. The grizzly was gone as quickly as it had come, but for several seconds, I could hear it huffing and crashing down into a draw below me.

Scared? Not at first—there wasn't time—but then my knees began to shake, and I decided it might be a good idea to leave. As I turned to go, no longer worrying about where the trail was, I noticed two piles of bear scat about 10 feet apart. The first was quite loose, typical of a bear that had been feeding on vegetation or meat. I wish I had taken time to examine it more closely. The elongated pellets in the second pile were firm and exactly the same color as the clay in the lick, indicating that the bear had indeed used the lick and had probably moved the rock.

This is what I think happened: The grizzly, which I assume was a male because of its large size, was waiting to ambush what it thought was a bugling bull elk that was approaching the lick. Instead of an elk, what finally arrived was an evil-smelling human being—me. This had to be very unnerving for the bear, and it, no doubt, became more nervous and agitated when I continued to dillydally around—leaving and coming back, then leaving and coming back the second time. The bear finally lost its cool and charged, but it veered off at the last second.

At camp that evening, while I braced my nerves, Aune added another possibility to the scenario. "The grizzly might already have killed an elk near the lick," he said, "and it was either feeding on or guarding the kill when you blundered into the area." The thought called for another bracer.

A shiver still runs through me when I realize the grizzly was probably crouched within 50 yards and watching me all the while I was at the lick. Perhaps that's why I felt so uneasy about the place. The thing I remember most was the bear's incredible speed. An elk using the lick wouldn't have had time to look up before the grizzly would have been on it. If the bear had decided to take me, I would not have had time enough to draw a revolver if I had been carrying one. I couldn't have gotten it out of the holster before the bear hit me. And "hit" is, no doubt, the right word. I've seen quite a few grizzly bears in Montana and in Alaska, and my impression was that this one was in the 500-pound class. At the rate it was going, being struck by this bear would have been like being hit by a truck.

There is no way of knowing the grizzly's intent—perhaps the charge was only a bluff from the beginning—but I have a hunch that if I had turned to run instead of facing it, the bear would have taken me.

I certainly don't intend to stop bowhunting during the rut, but I do believe some precautions are in order. Time may prove me wrong, but I think that one of the best defenses against grizzlies is a confident demeanor. Walk around like you own the place and aren't afraid of anything, and I believe the bears will have more respect for you. At least, I hope so. Act like a victim, and you're apt to become one. There is something about fear that animals can sense, and they are experts at reading body language.

With an adequate rifle in hand, I wouldn't worry at all, but many elk seasons during the bugling period are for bowhunters only. A grizzly can be killed by a well-placed arrow, but a bow is almost useless when it comes to stopping a charge. In Montana, where I hunt and where most of the few remaining grizzlies in the Lower 48 are found, it is ". . . unlawful to use firearms in any manner in the hunting or killing of any game animal during an archery-only season." That doesn't necessarily mean that it is unlawful to carry a firearm during a Montana bowhunting season. However, I don't feel right about doing so.

Another possible defense is an aerosol spray of the type used by postmen to repel dogs. Some sprays have been developed to repel bears. The active ingredient in many repellent sprays is capsaicin, which is a derivative of cayenne pepper. These sprays have been tested on grizzly bears, and some of them were found to be effective. I once used a repellent spray on a truculent black bear that approached to within five feet, and it worked fine. The bear ran a short distance, laid down, and started rubbing its eyes. When I ran into the same bear several days later, it showed more respect. About stopping a grizzly in full charge, though, I'd prefer not to be there.

When it comes to grizzlies, no defense is sure. This animal is smart enough, stealthy enough, fast enough, and powerful enough to catch and kill a mature bull elk, and if one is really determined to kill you, you probably don't stand a chance. Remember, to a hungry grizzly's ears, an elk bugle sounds like a dinner bell. If you can't cope with that, remember that there are a lot of places to hunt elk where grizzlies don't exist.

Outdoor Life, April 1987

In the Grizzly Zone

BY CHUCK ADAMS

At twelve yards,
things get a little cozy.

Something about cannibalism makes me a little uneasy in my soul. I'm not talking about explorers in stew pots here; I'm referring to the intraspecies snacking that goes on all the time among animals in the wild. It's perfectly natural, of course, for siblings to turn their rivals into lunch, but that doesn't change the fact that for us humans, the practice seems to violate all decency. Even when it's just a big trout feasting on its little brother.

When the cannibal in question is an Alaska brown bear, the whole scale of the drama changes. "Decency" doesn't really enter into it.

Several years ago, on an October bowhunt for brown bear, my guide, Brent Jones, and I came across a 250-pound juvenile brownie killed and partially eaten by a much larger bear. Around the chewed-up carcass were huge pad marks—back tracks 16 inches long, front tracks 10 inches wide—and the destruction of the surrounding area told the story of the hellacious battle that must have preceded the kill. The scene looked like some crude attempt at agriculture: a good acre of roto-tilled ground, dislodged rocks and tattered alders.

A few days later we found an even larger bear that had also been killed and eaten. Around the remains were those same tracks. We had a fratricidal maniac on our hands, and a big one at that.

As we glassed the surrounding landscape, we couldn't help wondering where "Old Bruno" was hanging out. I hadn't come to the Alaska Peninsula looking for a record bear—a respectable eight-footer would have been fine with me—but those colossal tracks sure were tempting.

FRESH BROWN BEAR TRACKS were easy to spot in the sand along the salmon-rich streams.

We were hunting in a five-mile-wide valley, flanked by 3,000-foot peaks and blanketed with chest-high grass and 10-foot alders. Several clear, gravelly streams—ideal spawning habitat for Pacific salmon—lay braided across the valley floor, moving toward the ocean five miles away. But even in this remote corner of the planet, the bears were skittish. The first two weeks of my 21-day hunt hadn't produced a single decent opportunity, and frustration was beginning to set in.

There was no question that there were plenty of bears around—I'd already tried to stalk six of them—but I couldn't get close enough for a shot. The two rifle hunters camped nearby didn't help, but more troubling were the mutilated corpses that big brown was leaving strewn around the valley floor. Hunting pressure and lingering human odor might put bears on high alert, but a big, bad-tempered bear in the area terrifies all others to distraction.

Mother Nature, meanwhile, had been on a roll of her own. October is usually the prime month for hunting browns—the weather is stable and the bears are concentrated on salmon streams near heavy cover, permitting stalking at close range. But fall had swept in like a low-level apocalypse: It rained every day, the salmon runs were weak and swollen streams washed whatever spent salmon there were back out to sea. The bears were wandering willy-nilly, sucking down ground squirrels, blueberries and carrion with equal zeal.

Close Encounters

On the second afternoon of the hunt, we were watching a blonde sow with two cubs dig for squirrels on a hillside when a gorgeous, eight-foot brownie popped out of the alders half a mile below us. The bear was exactly what I wanted—mature, dark brown and heavily furred with no scars on his hide. Brent figured he'd go at least 900 pounds.

The bear was moving fast, obviously looking for food, so we hustled after him on hands and knees through a brush-choked draw, and in sucking mud. Despite the heavy cover, we caught fleeting glimpses of the animal each time he waded a stream or crested a knob ahead of us. An hour later, two miles up the valley, we rounded a bush in full stride and nearly piled into the bear. He was five yards away, butt to us, shoveling blueberries into his mouth.

What happened next, happened fast.

A puff of wind tugged the back of my collar—the first contrary breeze all day. The bear whirled, growled and curled back his dark, rubbery lips. His canines were huge. He circled me on stiff legs, barely 20 feet away, huffing deep in his throat. A stronger gust of wind hit my neck, and with a startled, explosive "woof" the bear turned and fled. And since I was just standing there with my mouth hanging open, I wasn't sorry to see him go.

A week later, we had another close call. We were halfway across a gravel bar when Brent hissed, "Get down!" But there was nowhere to hide: The nearest cover was 30 yards away. A massive brown bear swaggered from the brush, sniffed the ground . . . then spotted us. He froze, staring right at us, his eyes fixed in disbelief. Then he stood upright, uncoiling to his full height of seven or eight feet.

It was the kind of shot a bowhunter dreams about—25 yards, chest exposed, a stationary target—but I didn't move a muscle. The bear knew where we were and he was facing directly at us. When hit, bears almost always run in the direction in which they're facing, and they accelerate from 0 to 40 in a heartbeat, leaving no time for a second shot. This one might let me draw, aim and release, but it didn't take a brain surgeon to figure out what might happen next. This was a bear that would take out its own mother.

The bear stared at me for a few seconds, dropped to all fours and nonchalantly lumbered away like a chocolate D-8 Caterpillar. Brent sighed and lowered his rifle, a battered .375 Model 70. Encounters like this are old hat to him, but he never trusts a brown bear.

Not that bowhunting brown bears is tantamount to a death wish, but it does have a whiff of exclusivity. Fewer than 40 brown bears, 40 grizzly bears and 20 polar bears have been harvested by bowhunters in the past 100 years. Still, it's significant that not one of those bears caused a deadly disaster. Bowhunting dangerous bears can be thrilling, but with the proper preparation it doesn't have to be foolhardy.

I had practiced with my 86-pound Hoyt compound bow until I could hit a tennis ball every time at 30 yards. I had also established a few safety rules for myself: never to shoot beyond 30 yards, never to shoot an alerted bear and never to shoot a bear facing in my direction. And if worse came to worst, I was with one of the calmest, most experienced backup men in the bear-guiding business.

The Final Stalk

October 15 dawned clear and cold—the first cloudless day of our hunt. We had seen 36 brown bears so far, including cubs, but I had yet to nock an arrow. Brent and I decided not to climb high and glass that morning; instead, we sneaked inland along a creek that flowed past our oceanside camp. The breeze was in our faces as we eased over gravel gleaming with early morning frost.

Two miles upstream, we rounded a bend and then dropped to our knees. A hundred yards off, a brown bear the size of a hippo was moving away from us through scattered clumps of brush. He was massive.

Brent hung back as I ducked under a cutbank and tiptoed ahead. The bear was searching for salmon, kicking up geysers of spray as he crossed and recrossed the foot-deep water. He was moving fast—three or four miles per hour—and it was all I could do to stay within 200 yards.

Suddenly the bear froze, peered into the water and flipped out a two-foot silver salmon. He chomped down on the sashimi, shook off water like a dog and eased into a thicket. The wind was still right, so I shuffled ahead and stopped where the bear had disappeared. The muddy tracks were unmistakable—I'd found my cannibal.

I nocked an arrow and eased into the silence of the brush, my senses registering each flapping leaf, each micro-shift of the wind. Then I heard him, or rather it—salmon bones snapping between powerful jaws. The bear stood up 25 yards ahead, turned and swaggered directly toward me. He disappeared in a dip, and then loomed up behind the last alder bush between us. When he veered broadside I drew my bow; then he stepped into the clear. A perfect, broadside shot at 12 yards.

The bowstring sent my arrow through 10 inches of hide and muscle just behind the bear's right shoulder. I knew Brent was 30 or 40 yards behind me with the rifle, but I was not prepared for what happened next. The bear rose to his full height and let out a roar that would have steamed my glasses if I'd been wearing any. He looked directly down at me, not one twig between us, his head as wide as a garbage can lid and his lips curled back in pain and confusion. My thoughts at that moment are unprintable.

The bear was dead, but he didn't know it yet. He towered over me for three or four seconds, and then, thank God, he thundered away, emitting a bloodcurdling blast each time he hit the ground. We found him 160 paces away, all 1,400 pounds of him. And with his passing, several dozen lesser bears in the valley suddenly grew bolder.

Outdoor Life, August 1996

Black Bear Addiction

BY BOB ROBB

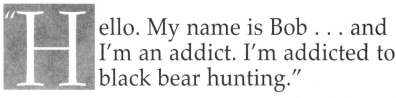

*Once you've had some
success, the odds are
you'll keep coming back
for more . . . and more.*

"Hello. My name is Bob . . . and I'm an addict. I'm addicted to black bear hunting."

It's true. I spend far too much time planning and executing bear hunts each year. I can't get enough of it. And the reason has little to do with success. The root of my addiction is that bear hunting challenges my skills in every way possible. Scouting, planning, stalking, stealth, woodcraft, shooting—everything. It all comes into play when you're bear hunting.

I've hunted them about every way you can. In spring, I run bait stations near my home in Alaska. While many of my friends are off chasing turkeys somewhere in the lower 48, I'm scouting new bait sites or spending time spot-and-stalk-hunting bears on the steep, vibrant green mountainsides. I've endured bad weather and rough seas boating on the Alaskan coast, spotting bears as they gorge themselves on everything from fresh grasses to carrion. In fall, I always spend at least a week hunting bears—usually the technique is spot-and-stalk again, but sometimes I'll be following the sound of hounds as they chase bears up, down and around the steepest, thickest terrain imaginable. One thing I can definitely say about hunting bears: It's not boring!

Population Explosion

Black bear populations are on the upswing across North America. While counting bears is anything but an exact science, estimates in 1988 put the number at 902,000, with 512,000 in Canada and 390,000 in the U.S. That's a huge increase from the estimated total of 550,000 bears in the U.S. and Canada in 1977. And they're showing up in places where bears never were before. Maryland, for example, now counts some 200 bruins. Nevada reports an increase from 24 in 1977 to 300 in 1992; North Dakota from none to 250; even Oklahoma has gone from zero to 25. California's numbers have also skyrocketed.

There are several reasons for this growth. Improved habitat is a major one. But so is a shift in attitude toward bears: It has gone from allowing the wholesale killing of bears during the height of the fur-trade era in the 19th century to classifying them as "varmints" with bounties on their heads, to designating them in all states as a big-game animal with restricted seasons and controlled harvests. The establishment of protected parklands in the late 19th and early 20th centuries—among them Great Smoky Mountain National Park, Everglades National Park in Florida and Adirondack State Park in New York—also gave bears places where they could flourish. And flourish they have.

Odds for Success

Fall bear hunting is, as they say, the same, only different. It all depends on where you are. But no matter how you choose to hunt bears, it will be more challenging than deer hunting. Pennsylvania, for example, is a state with a reputation for good bear hunting. Yet there are only an estimated 8,000 bears in the Keystone State, compared with more than a million deer. Gary Alt, a Pennsylvania wildlife biologist and nationally recognized black bear expert, cites a survey of his state's hunters disclosing that 13 percent of successful bear hunters killed the first black bear they had ever seen in the wild. Moreover, only 53 percent of the surveyed hunters had seen more than six bears in their entire lifetimes—which in many instances included trips to places such as Yellowstone National Park. The point is, if you don't have a game plan and knowledge of local bear habits and haunts, you might as well spend your time looking for a four-leaf clover.

The Food Factor

Regardless of where you hunt, remember one thing: A black bear is a large, furred food processor. Its movements and habits are largely dictated by an insatiable appetite. Not only that, but black bears tend to concentrate on specific food sources at specific times. Generally speaking, their preferred fall food sources are berries, mast crops and fruits, though you can add migrating salmon to the list if you hunt coastal areas in the Pacific Northwest and Alaska.

Your first step as a hunter should be to call a state game biologist

GUNS AND LOADS

BLACK BEARS CAN BE TAKEN WITH MOST STANDARD DEER-HUNTING CARTRIDGES OR BOWHUNTING SET-UPS. USE STOUT BULLETS FOR BOTH CONTROLLED EXPANSION AND PENETRATION. HERE ARE MY CHOICES:

Rifles: Cartridges in the .270, .30/06 and 7mm Magnum class are excellent for hunting from coast to coast. I like .30 caliber and up for the larger wound channel, and have found that .35 caliber cartridges such as the .358 Winchester and .35 Whelen are superb.

Handguns: Single-shot specialty pistols such as the Thompson/Center Encore, Remington XP-100 and Savage Striker in cartridges such as 7x30 Waters, .308 Winchester and similar rounds work very well. Revolvers in .41 Magnum, .44 Magnum and .454 Casull are effective, too.

Muzzleloaders: My personal minimum is .50 caliber, but I prefer a .54 caliber. Use conical or, where legal, sabot-encased conical bullets weighing at least 300 grains.

Bows and Arrows: Use broadheads with super-sharp blades and arrows tuned for dart-like flight. The new fiber-optic bowsights make precision arrow placement much easier than with metal pins, especially when shooting at the black hide of a bear on the cusp of daylight.

and ask about the preferred foods in the area you plan to hunt. In many mountainous western states, for example, huckleberries draw bears like magnets. In California and Oregon, I've watched bears tear up manzanita patches and almost knock down laurel trees to get at their berries. In the Southwest, black bears eat acorns like candy and routinely flatten large patches of prickly pear cactus. In the East, acorns are a key food source, along with beechnuts, chokecherries, hazelnuts and black cherries. Fruit orchards, especially apples, also draw bruins, as does skunk cabbage.

Keep in mind that bears do not act like deer. That is, when one specific food source has been depleted, they'll move on until they find another. While deer may use an acorn ridge for a month, bears may be on it a week or less before leaving. Bears are very mobile animals, too. Alt's research shows that some males will use an area as big as 60 square miles as their home range, moving all over it, looking for food. Females in the study generally confined themselves to 15 square miles.

The Value of Scouting

Anyone who takes a black bear without scouting ought to buy a lottery ticket. If they're that lucky, they'll probably win $200 million. To give yourself a realistic chance at getting a black bear, don't look just to food sources; also keep an eye out for scat, tracks and signs of feeding activity—such as overturned rocks, dug-up anthills, decaying logs that have been torn up and places where bears have literally ripped branches from trees to get at the nuts. If possible, also ask local sportsmen questions about recent bear sightings, areas where bears are seen from year to year and so on.

In the Southwest, I often scout for deer and bears during the summer. While I glass early mornings and late evenings for deer, I'll spend the middays checking out oak groves and cactus patches. If I find trees with limbs torn off during the previous fall, I can be reasonably sure that bears will be in the area when these same trees produce next fall's nut crop.

Hunting Tactics

Bears move primarily at night, though you can catch them out during the day if they're not heavily pressured. I've found that late evening is by far the best time to take a bear. Bears prefer to travel

SEVEN SUREFIRE WAYS TO FIELD-JUDGE BEARS

HOW CAN YOU TELL IF A BLACK BEAR IS A BIG BLACK BEAR? AFTER ALL, BEARS DON'T HAVE EASILY IDENTIFIABLE FEATURES, SUCH AS ANTLERS. WHILE THERE IS NO SUBSTITUTE FOR THE EXPERIENCE OF LOOKING AT LOTS OF BEARS, HERE ARE SEVEN TIPS THAT WILL HELP YOU JUDGE THEIR SIZE, EVEN ON YOUR FIRST HUNT.

1. **Ears:** Big bears appear to have small ears, because their heads are so large. Generally, a record book-class black bear will have ears that measure at least eight inches apart from tip to tip.

2. **Body Length:** A female will rarely exceed $5^{1}/_{2}$ feet in length. Mature males are longer than that, however, with many trophy-class bears often more than six feet from nose to tail.

3. **Front Feet:** Measure the track of a front pad, add one, change the inches to feet and you have the approximate size the bear's hide will square. Thus, a $5^{1}/_{2}$-inch pad will carry a $6^{1}/_{2}$-foot boar. Females rarely have front paws that exceed $4^{1}/_{2}$ inches in length.

4. **Beer Belly:** Even in spring, a big male will have a huge belly that will almost brush the ground when he walks. Young bears have smaller bellies.

5. **Snout:** Big bears have what appears to be a short snout. Younger bears and females have what appears to be a longish, pointed snout.

6. **Height:** A larger-than-average bear, when standing on all fours, will have a back line that reaches to or above the waist of an average-sized man.

7. **Cubs:** Boars hate cubs. If there are cubs with a larger bear, it's a female. If the cubs scamper up a tree and the female begins to act nervous, get ready, a boar may be in the area.

just before dark, feed at night, then retreat to the nastiest, thickest stuff around to bed for the day. Swamps, cool, timbered ridges and overgrown clear-cuts are where they most like to bed. Stationing yourself between a bedding area and a food source is a great way to get a shot.

In the inter-mountain West, I like to pick a spot where I can see a lot of country, and then glass. Forget about looking for bear sign, though. If there's food around—berries, nuts—and it's a good bear area, sooner or later you'll spot a bear. Look mostly along the edges of timber and thick brush. In the thicker country of the East and Midwest, scout and find sign, then hunt it as you would a deer, still-hunting or taking up stand in a good-looking area.

Never underestimate a bear's sense of smell. You must get the wind right, or forget it. I've had bears smell me at half a mile and bolt as if hit with an electrical shock. Always approach the core of your hunting area and take your spotting station from downwind. Bears also have excellent hearing, so wear quiet clothing, try not to make any strange noises and take pains to quietly stalk in for your shot.

A black bear's Achilles' heel is its eyesight. Though it is poor by our standards, don't assume it's Mr. Magoo-like. While I've had bears see me at 100 yards, if you wear drab clothing and don't move when they're looking your way, chances are they won't figure out what you are.

Regardless of your weapon, try to take any bear through both lungs. I've never seen a double-lunged black bear go more than 100 yards. Aim to place your bullet or broadhead behind the front leg. Bears have thick hides and lots of fat and don't usually leave much of a blood trail to follow. If your shot placement is a bit off, be prepared for a long and difficult tracking job.

When you do everything right, however, and finally get a thick-furred 200-pound-plus bear on the ground, you have every right to be proud, because you've done something that few other hunters have: taken one of North America's true trophy animals. You may even have become addicted.

Outdoor Life, October 1998

LEGENDARY
BIG-GAME
HUNTS

LEGENDARY BIG-GAME HUNTS

Kenai Moose and Black Bear

BY RUSSELL ANNABEL

Thirty days
on the Chickaloon.

It came to pass that in the twilight of a September evening we hazed a string of packhorses down the west slope of the Kenai hills and made camp at nightfall in a grove of tall cottonwoods on the bank of the Chickaloon River.

There were three of us, Gunn Buckingham, a sportsman from Memphis, Tenn.; Rolland Osborne, seventeen-year-old combination cook and wrangler; and myself, the guide. We had outfitted at Moose Pass Station, Mile 29 on the Alaska Railroad, and had come down the peninsula by way of the old Russian trail leading up Devil's Creek and across the forks of the Resurrection Creek. We were after moose and black bear, and planned to remain in the field at least thirty days.

A short distance below our camp in the cottonwoods the Kenai hills melted down into an immense reach of marshland—the Chickaloon flats—which is unquestionably the finest, or at least one of the finest, summer moose ranges on earth. At this season of the year, when the nights were getting frosty and the flies had disappeared, the moose were coming up into the timberline pastures for the beginning of the rutting period, with the cows and yearlings in the lead and the old bulls following a few days behind.

On the morning after our arrival Buckingham and I saddled up and rode down to a birch-covered ridge on the margin of the great flat. About an hour after leaving camp, while riding through the close-packed trees, we saw a large black bear on a hillside ahead of us. He was in an opening, and there was just time for a shot before he would cross it and enter a tangle of alder bushes. Buckingham dismounted and pulled his rifle, a .270 Model 54 Winchester, out of its saddle boot.

"Think you can hit him?" I asked. The bear was about 350 yards distant.

"Reckon I'll try a shot for luck," he said.

I'd have bet money right then that the bear was going to get away without a scratch. Three hundred and fifty yards is a long shot at game in any man's country; and this bear was moving along the hillside at a good pace and was partially concealed by a stand of tall red-top grass. But I kept quiet, as a good guide should, and focused my glasses on the animal in order to call Buckingham's shot.

He lay down prone, spent a moment fussing with his Lyman sight, adjusted his sling strap, and fired just as the bear reached the edge of the bushes. I saw the grass weave under the muzzle blast; saw a spurt of gray rock dust puff up behind the bear; but I could not tell for certain whether he was hit or not. It was mighty close, though, and Buckingham's stock took a rise in my estimation. The bear turned, leaped a shallow gully, and started galloping back the way he had come. Buckingham grumbled something under his breath as he cast the exploded cartridge. Then—

Wham!—the little .270 crashed out again. This time I heard the indescribable slap of the bullet striking flesh. The bear stopped, half turned to face us, sagged slowly against the hillside, and suddenly came rolling end over end. A pretty bit of rifle work. I held out my hand to Buckingham in token of apology and congratulation. "You sure fetched him with that second shot," I said admiringly.

"Shucks," he said. "The first one was too far back—through the flanks. I pulled off, I guess."

And when I rolled the bear, a toothless old male, out of the rock pile he had come to rest in, I found two bullet holes in him—one through the flanks and the other through the lungs. The appropriate observation will occur to the reader without my writing it.

The bear measured six feet seven inches from nose to tail: not a record, but one of the largest I had ever seen. We loaded the pelt, skull and tenderloins on my saddle horse and returned to camp. The game trails we crossed on the way back were cut up with fresh moose tracks, and twice we saw spruce saplings which had been stripped of bark and limbs by some bull rubbing his antlers against them.

In the afternoon, while Rolland fleshed the bear pelt and cleaned the skull, Buckingham and I climbed a hill behind camp and killed a half dozen willow ptarmigan. The birds were just changing into winter plumage and their piebald coloring, brown and speckled white, gave them a curious camouflaged appearance against the green hillside. They were little giants of vitality. Two of them, shot through the breast with .22 longs, flew nearly to the base of the hill before they dropped. Another, shot through the head, rocketed straight up, spun for a moment in an erratic circle, then set its wings and sailed a few yards into a clump of alders.

Just before sundown that evening we located seven moose browsing on a little plateau about five miles down the valley. At least three of them were bulls. In the slant rays of the sun their polished antlers gleamed like heliograph mirrors. At this time of year the bulls are the most conspicuous animals in the hills, the flash of their antlers in the sunlight often betraying them to the naked eye at a distance too great to pick out their bodies even with binoculars.

The next morning, September 28, broke, clear and cold, with a steady wind blowing in from the ocean. We rose early, and after an imperial breakfast of broiled ptarmigan breasts and bear steaks, saddled up and rode down to the plateau on which we had seen the seven moose. There was not an animal in sight, but I figured they were sleeping in a jack-spruce grove close by. We circled for the wind and approached the place slowly. I didn't want to jump them unexpectedly if I could help it; there is nothing more awkward than trying to pick the best head out of several stampeding bull moose. We crossed the head of a grassy swale and rode down to the point of the jack-spruce grove.

Suddenly my horse, a spooky Oregon cayuse, threw up his head and snorted. We reined in and dismounted. Presently, swaggering through the emerald shadows under the trees, came an ancient bull. Ribbons and tatters of velvet dangled from his gnarled and twisted antlers. He was grizzled, sway-backed and lean. As he poked along he uttered deep, chesty grunts—Aghr-r-ugh, aghr-r-ugh.

It is a fact that bull moose aren't particularly bright during the rutting season. This old fellow was no exception. We walked along behind him, leading our horses, for 100 yards without attracting so much as a suspicious glance. Maybe he thought we were just two more moose. When he reached the denser part of the spruce grove, Buckingham and I tied our horses and followed more cautiously. In a moment he turned into a tiny opening, a sort of moss-carpeted arena. Here we witnessed a most curious sight.

Our ancient bull swaggered—he really tottered, I suppose, but there was a comical air of bravado about his progress—into the opening. Then, presto! there were four moose instead of one. A cow and two young bulls had come out from the timber on the opposite side to meet him. At once the trio of bulls began maneuvering about with obvious belligerent intent. As none of the heads was worth taking, I got out my camera and prayed there would be light enough to get pictures of the battle royal that seemed imminent. But no combat occurred.

After a good deal of grunting and a number of warlike movements they suddenly jammed their antlers together with a clash and stood as motionless as statues. So closely was the pile of antlers interfretted that it was actually impossible at fifty yards to tell for certain which antler belonged to which bull. The cow walked around them once or twice, apparently quite as curious and interested as we, and then went off to nibble at some alder twigs. I didn't look at my watch, but we must have waited where we were for at least a quarter of an hour. When we left, they were still standing with their heads together. Buckingham suggested that the ancient one was probably imparting some of the facts of life to the other two.

Late in the afternoon we jumped four moose in a hillside burn—a yearling, three cows and a bull. The bull, a young fellow with a set of antlers that was almost in the trophy class, sported a splendid bell. It hung twenty inches or more below his throat. Old bulls with heavy, wide-spreading antlers almost never have bells of any length. I don't know whether they simply disappear with age or whether they freeze off during hard winters or are torn off in fights.

The next day, about four o'clock in the afternoon, we killed another black bear. We had crossed over a high summit to the head of a valley that ran down to another watershed, had seen several moose, none of which Buckingham wanted, and had started back to camp when the bear walked into the trail about 200 yards ahead of us. Buckingham tumbled off his horse and opened fire. At the first shot the bear started down the mountain like a streak. The second shot went wide, ricocheting off a slab of shale. Buckingham said something unfit for publication even in expurgated form. Then he knelt, pulled another bead on the bounding animal and managed, just as it crashed into the edge of an alder clump, to get in a finishing shot.

In this bear, as in the first one, the entrails were reduced to an unrecognized pulp by the 130-grain bullets. I had read an article in an issue of *Outdoor Life* praising the .270 Winchester but had never seen it tried on game before this hunt. It is all that was claimed for it. I have since seen it used on sheep, goat, caribou and Kodiak bear, and one properly placed shot always brings down the game with neatness and dispatch.

It was nearly dark when we got back to camp with the pelt. Rolland had a steaming, savory and most welcome rabbit stew waiting for us. He had shot the rabbits—low-bush moose, he called them—with my .22 pistol that morning while rounding up the horses.

The following week we were in the saddle each day from dawn till dusk, riding up first one creek then another. The rut was in full swing now, and there were moose everywhere. Buckingham passed up so many fine bulls that I began to suspect he was out for a record-breaking trophy and would be satisfied with nothing smaller.

The morning of October 5 came in full of sun and sweet mountain breeze. A shift of snow had fallen during the night and there was a keen tingle in the air, as if it were strained through ice. The cottonwoods in the bottoms had turned yellow; aspens were flaming on the ridge crests; Arctic heather smouldered blood red among the rough-strewn boulders on the hillsides. When we woke at daybreak this morning a great flight of sandhill cranes were circling above the hills, their wild, chuckling cries coming as clear as bell notes through the frosty atmosphere.

After breakfast we put up a lunch and rode across the range to the valley in which we had killed the second black bear. About three o'clock in the afternoon, while riding along the edge of an old burn, we saw our Kenai bull. He was standing back in a strip of spruce timber intersecting the burn and was rubbing his antlers against a sapling. It was hard to obtain a good view of him, but even a glimpse sufficed to convince us that he ranked high as a trophy—far and away the finest bull we had seen. He was late out of the velvet and the upper surfaces of his antlers gleamed under the trees like polished ivory. The blades looked broad and massive, and it seemed to me, from the fleeting sight I had of them, that they were fitted out with a wonderful array of spikes.

We tied our horses in an alder thicket and started toward him for a closer inspection. The wind was right and the stalk seemed a comparatively simple matter. The only trouble was the bed of a dry pond that intervened between us and the timber. Coarse, dry grass, which made a terrific rustling and crunching under foot, was standing here. There was no way to avoid it, either; from any other angle of approach the wind would be wrong. So we crossed over as best we could, aware that we made enough noise to frighten an alert bull half out of his wits.

After a dozen paces into the timber I knew the stalk had gone wrong. The bull had moved deeper into the gloom of the trees. As the strip of timber was not more than fifty yards wide, I expected he would leave it from the opposite side and run out across the open burn. We ran to head him off, careless of noise now that we believed he knew of our presence—hoping only for a look at him before he was too far away.

The thrill of the stalk with a possible kill as its object had suddenly taken hold on Buckingham, and he sprinted after me through the bushes with surprising energy. We broke into the open, and came to a dismayed halt. No bull. Well, then he was still back in the timber and probably had not heard us at all.

We commenced working upwind through the spruces, with elaborate caution now. The bull having eluded us twice, we were sure he was the veritable Pearl of the Kenai. Buckingham played Uncas to my Hawk-Eye, putting his shoepacs down with a softness and precision that could not have failed to win a nod of approval from the grim old Sagamore himself. He carried the .270 at ready, with his thumb curled under the safety catch.

After five minutes of such progress, with the end of the timber almost in sight, I began to wonder if the bull might not have doubled back and entered the burn on the other side. By this time I would have taken oath that he was a Field Museum specimen. The thought of losing through a blundered stalk the only moose Buckingham had shown any real interest in, was gall and wormwood. My professional vanity, I thought, was going to be reduced in amperage after this affair. (Why the merry Hades hadn't I persuaded Buckingham to shoot when we first saw the bull, taking a chance on his being a good trophy? Then there would at least have been an alibi in the outcome.)

Well, we were nearly to the end of the timber. There was one thing left to do—separate, on the off chance the bull was on one or the other side of the burn and still in sight. If Buck saw him he could judge the head for himself and try his luck if it suited him. If I saw him, I could return and try to find Buckingham in time to get him back for a shot. Dismal prospect. Then—A brown shade showed through a tracery of low-hanging boughs. Although motionless and formless, it was a color our eyes had learned to distinguish and register automatically. It was the bull. He was standing in a pool of deep shadow, and behind him were a cow and a yearling. The cow was looking straight at us, with her great ears turned forward and her bright little eyes staring hard. Only the superb indifference of the bull kept her from headlong flight.

The bull swung his head slowly from side to side. He grunted: Aghr-r-r-ugh, aghr-r-r-ugh. That was moose talk. He was telling his lady what a great fellow he was, and what he'd do to any presumptious young upstart bull who dared come within half a mile of her. He was modestly requesting her to observe that he was carrying the widest and heaviest spread of antlers that had yet come up Chickaloon River from the marshes—and please notice the number of points and pothooks, my dear, and the really exquisite symmetry of these brow antlers.

I had my 12-power glasses trained on him from a distance somewhat less than fifty yards and could see that he was a fine trophy. But I hesitated. He was facing away from us, and somehow that always makes a game head appear larger than it really is. I waited until he swung broadside: then I was convinced.

"Take him, Buck!" I whispered.

The .270 came up, wavered on line for a heartbeat, held steady as a rock. Wham! A spurt of orange licked out against the shadows and the muzzle blast made the leaves dance. The bull slewed sidewise, half fell, then caught himself and staggered after the cow, who was already in full flight. The shot had taken him too far back: it had missed the chest cavity.

Again the shadows flickered as Buckingham's rifle crashed out. This time the bull went to his knees. His great head was in the grass; he groaned abysmally, drew up one long foreleg in a last struggle to rise. Midway of the movement he died, and rolled over.

A noble kill, lying there in the wind-dried grass and the fragrant Hudson Bay tea bushes. We stretched a steel tape across his antlers and gaped at the reading—sixty-nine inches. He would be a lucky hunter who took a larger head out of Alaska this year... Tomorrow we would bring all the horses to the carcass and pack in the hide, head and meat. Perhaps the meat would keep long enough to permit packing it out to the railroad, where we could give it to the Indian school at Seward. An odd thing to think about—white men packing meat to husky young natives while they learned about algebra and toothbrushes.

I started taking off the head and cape. When I had worked down to the brisket on both sides, I straightened up to let the kink out of my back and to sharpen my knife. At that moment Buck gave a startled exclamation and dove for his rifle, which stood against a tree several yards distant.

TAKING OFF THE CAPE. This picture was snapped just before the grizzly bear arrived on the scene.

Looking hastily over my shoulder I saw—by all the Red Gods—a three-year-old grizzly. He was not a hundred feet away and was ambling nonchalantly toward us, straight into the wind reeking of smokeless powder, blood and man scent.

I heard Buckingham's rifle bolt rattle, and an instant later the shot, fired directly behind me, nearly exploded my ear drums. The hollow-point bullet struck the bear with a smart whoo-oup, and I knew that this shot also was too far back to kill immediately. The grizzly went down, however, bawling, somersaulting and tearing up the moss. Buck fired again—and missed; he ran forward a few paces as the bear rolled behind a windfall.

Then, whang!—a third shot. The grizzly was still very much alive. Buck cast the empty cartridge just as the wounded animal gained his feet and made off in a crazy, stammering gallop. The next sound that broke the quiet was a metallic click: the .270 was empty of cartridges. Upshot: the bear escaped. Moral: keep the magazine of your rifle filled.

Back to camp in the clear Alaskan dusk. A mere bronze shaving of a new moon rose as we topped the summit and looked down upon the valley in which our camp was pitched. Far below, in the shadowy cottonwoods, we could discern the soft, luminous glow of the candle-lit tent walls. A thin stratum of wood smoke, shot through with starlight, hung like a purple veil above the trees.

As we worked down the slope, letting our horses pick their own way over the loose shale, Buckingham began to sing. The hunt was over, and it had been one to remember. It was marred only by thoughts of the grizzly lying out somewhere in the alders with a couple of bullet holes blasted through him. Perhaps he got well. I hope that he did, and that he will remember never again to walk into the wind when it carries man scent. Perhaps we'll meet him on the Chickaloon burn another autumn day.

Outdoor Life, March 1933

The Caribou

BY JACK O'CONNOR

A creature of glacier and tundra, he's the world's handsomest big-game animal— and he can be one of the most rattle-brained.

No more beautiful big-game animal than a bull caribou walks the face of the earth. With his towering, heavily palmated antlers with their many points, his snowy neck, his flaring nostrils, his sleek, seal-brown body, he is a gorgeous sight, the very epitome of the wild and uninhabited northland of mountain and glacier and tundra.

He is a handsomer animal than even the African kudu or sable, more regal than the wild sheep or the elk. For looks alone, the only creature that might shade him is the great gold and black tiger.

If he were as smart as he is beautiful, the caribou would be one of the world's great trophies, but he is, alas, a comparatively dumb and rattle-brained creature. At least he has been in the fall months when I have hunted him. During the rut, a bull caribou is the goofiest, most self-destructive large animal I have ever seen—even worse than a love-crazed mule deer, and that is saying a lot. To an amorous bull caribou everything looks like a cow caribou, even a packhorse with a white pack cover on top of a pile of bedrolls and panniers.

One afternoon in September, 1951, when my son Bradford and I were packing over a big rounded hill above timberline in northern British Columbia, we were in typical caribou country and had seen some of the animals at a distance. Then two big bulls showed up, one with a perfectly tremendous head with the largest shovel I have ever seen. They were convinced that the weary horses in our packstring were a herd of cow caribou. They'd come trotting up to investigate, catch the man smell, and go prancing off. Then they'd look back, see the horses, think they were cows once more, forget what had frightened them, and come bouncing back. They did this several times, and I busily took still pictures and movies of them. But the horses were getting nervous, and finally one of our guides chased the bulls off. Caribou season did not open until the next day, but Bradford was dying to knock over that gorgeous bull. I refused to let him shoot. He later got a bull that was as good if not better—and it was entirely legal.

Our caribou are simply North American reindeer. Like many of our other large game animals, they crossed over from Asia by the land bridge, which existed across the Bering Strait for hundreds of thousands of years and was finally covered by the sea only about 15,000 years ago. They are found all over the arctic and subarctic from northern Norway to Greenland, and they are likewise found far south along the high Rockies wherever altitude creates large portions of arctic climate and vegetation above timberline. I have seen many hundreds along the British Columbia-Alberta border in the timberline country on the crest of the Rockies, and I have seen equal numbers near the snow peaks and glaciers of the western Yukon.

In the southern part of their range, caribou often live in heavy forest in country below timberline. There are some of this breed in southern British Columbia, a few in northern Idaho, and possibly some in Washington and Montana. However, typical caribou ground is the tundra country of the arctic prairies and the similar country above and near timberline in the high mountains—a country of arctic willow, dwarf birch, and caribou moss, of glacier and snowfields, of muskeg and little meandering streams full of grayling.

Caribou are cold-country animals, and they seldom are found far from perpetual snow. Their coats are so warm that even on a nippy fall day, when the hunter is shivering in wool pants and down jacket, the caribou will be lying on glaciers and snow patches to keep cool.

During the ice age, caribou ranged much farther south than they do now. Their bones and horns are found in Pleistocene deposits far down in the United States, and in Europe our gifted Cro-Magnon ancestors not only hunted them but also drew beautiful pictures of them on the walls of their caves.

I have done all of my caribou hunting in the mountains of western and northern Canada, and to me caribou country means rolling hills above timberline—country so high and cold that there are snow patches in the hollows and on the north side of the hills, and where there are glaciers in the higher mountains.

Caribou generally range in lower, more rounded mountains than sheep, but many times I have found caribou on the same hill with Stone and Dall sheep. The first bull caribou I ever saw was alone in a basin with a large herd of bighorns. However, the caribou is not nearly so adaptable an animal as the wild sheep. The bighorn, whose ancestors also crossed the ice-sheathed land bridge across the Bering Strait, gradually moved south and established himself in subtropical Arizona and Sonora, but caribou must have their ice and their tundra.

The British believe that all the caribou of the world are of the same species, and that the various forms of caribou are simply subspecies. Americans generally divide the caribou of North America into three species—the woodland caribou of eastern Canada and Maine, the mountain caribou of the Rockies, and the Barren Ground caribou of the arctic prairies. As Americans are great dividers and classifiers, they have further divided these three species into various subspecies, but it seems to me that these subdivisions are so much hairsplitting. If, for instance, there is any difference between the mountain caribou of British Columbia's Cassiar Mountains and the Barren Ground caribou 200 miles away in the Yukon, I fail to see what it is. I have seen pictures of wild reindeer shot in the Norwegian arctic, and to me they look just like caribou. Seton's *Lives of Game Animals* lists eight subspecies of the Barren-Ground caribou alone.

Barren Ground caribou of the far north average smaller than either the woodland or the mountain caribou. However, some of the Barren Ground animals have wonderful heads. The best heads I have ever seen were in the Cassiar district of northwest British Columbia, and possibly the heaviest animals I have run into were in the Smoky River country of Alberta. To the layman's eyes, anyway, a caribou is a caribou, from the glaciers of Norway to the Barren Grounds of Canada.

The caribou is unique in the deer family in that the cows have antlers, but there is little difficulty in telling bulls from cows because the antlers of the cows are spindly little things whereas those of the bulls are enormous. In addition, mature bulls have white necks and are much larger than the cows. A big bull mountain caribou is almost as large as a young bull elk, but a cow is about the size of a mule deer.

In late August and in September, when they are generally hunted, the caribou are getting their new winter coat. The hair is a dark, grayish-brown, with the coarse and springy outer hairs overlaying a coat of fine, warm wool. The necks of the bulls range from creamy white to a light gray, which looks white at a distance. Often this white neck hair extends clear back on the shoulders. It is my impression that the neck hair of the Barren Ground bulls is lighter than that of the Osborn caribou of the British Columbia Cassiars and much lighter than that of the caribou in the Smoky River country of Alberta. The hairs of a caribou's coat are hollow, and as a consequence caribou are great swimmers and float as if they were wearing life preservers. This coat is one of the warmest in nature, and before down sleeping bags became common in the far north, the trappers and Indians used caribou hides for winter sleeping robes. Even today in their winter camps they use caribou hides to floor their tents

The ears of the caribou are small and heavily haired, and the gray of the head turns brown at the hairy muzzle. The legs are brown in front and on the sides, white in back. The tail is white, and a frightened caribou throws it up when it starts off, just as the whitetail deer does.

The caribou is built for the deep snow and the mucky ground of the arctic. His legs are long and his hoofs large and circular. When the caribou is in a soft bog or in snow, the bearing surface of his hoof is increased by his bringing more of the foot against the ground. The tracks show as two widespread half-moons with the imprint of the patterns behind. The whole footprint of the caribou will be around four inches wide and seven or eight inches long. It is if he were walking on snowshoes, and he can cross without difficulty boggy country where a heavy, small-footed animal like a horse or an elk would have difficulty. Oddly enough, the addax, a beautiful antelope that dwells in the sands of North Africa's Sahara Desert, has, through thousands of years of dwelling in soft sands, developed a foot much like that of the caribou.

A curious thing about the hoof of the caribou is that it clicks as the animal walks, and authorities say the click takes place within the hoof as the weight is taken off but before it is lifted from the ground. I have never seen a big migration of caribou, but I first heard this clicking one time in the Yukon when I was high in a pass above the St. Claire River hunting white sheep. A little herd of cow and calf caribou traveling from one drainage to another came trotting by me not over 50 feet away, and I could hear this clicking as they passed.

Bud Helmericks, the arctic guide and explorer, tells me that caribou have very good ears, and that in the winter when snowshoes squeak on dry snow they are exceedingly hard to stalk. But in the fall when I have hunted them, they have always struck me as being very easy to stalk, just as long as the hunter watched the wind. Their eyes are very poor, certainly no better than those of a grizzly bear and maybe not as good. Many times I have got close to caribou simply by walking slowly upwind in plain sight but taking care to make no sudden movements.

It does not pay to take undue chances in stalking any animal, but if the caribou hunter doesn't have much cover, he shouldn't worry unduly about it. One time I was hunting exactly on the Alberta-British Columbia boundary in what was then wonderful mountain caribou country around a mountain that is perfectly flat on top. In the Southwest it would be called a mesa, but up there it had been given the names Coffin Top and Casket Mountain. A Cree guide named Isaac Plante and I came over a ridge one day to see a whole great basin filled with caribou—cows, calves, and big bulls.

The rut was just beginning, and the animals were restless. Several large bulls were in sight, and the best one was a fine big fellow with heavy antlers and double shovels. The wind was right in our faces as Isaac and I started moving slowly down the hill toward the bull. We were within 400 yards of him when suddenly he threw his head up and took off at right angles with his long, springy trot. We saw the last of him as he disappeared over a ridge about a mile away.

I knew the bull couldn't have smelled us because we had the wind right, and as far as I could tell there was no way he could have seen us. "What made that bull run?" I asked Isaac, disappointed.

"Nothing made him run," he told me. "He's just crazy. All caribou do crazy things."

The next best bull in sight had very long antlers with little shovel development and not much more palmation than an elk's—a type of antler, incidentally, which is quite common among the mountain caribou of the Smoky River country. The bull was lying on a little snow patch gazing off into space. There was no cover anywhere near, so Isaac and I simply walked slowly and quietly toward him.

When we were about 200 or 250 yards away, we sat on the hillside, looked him over with glasses, and decided to take him at our leisure. Then a couple of cows came prancing up to pay a social call on the bull. He got to his feet politely, but it looked as though he seemed a bit puzzled about the whole business.

Bored and disappointed at the bull's indifference, the cows started looking around. Presently they spied us and apparently decided we had an odd look. But, like all caribou, they wanted to check with their noses what their eyes had told them. They made a circle until they caught our wind. Then they jumped into the air, hoisted their tails and took off at a high trot. The big bull had been watching them, and when he saw those tails go up he also started off. But I'd been anticipating the move. I swung the crosswires in my scope along ahead of him, squeezed the trigger, and the 130-grain, .270 bullet struck right behind his shoulder, passing through his lungs. He was instantly down, and I don't think he kicked more than twice.

Isaac and I went down to take some pictures of the bull, skin out the head, and quarter the carcass so we could come back for it with a packhorse. We forgot all about the big bull with the double shovels and were hard at work. Suddenly, there he was, running directly toward us, great antlers laid back almost to his rump, lifting his knees in that beautiful, springy trot typical of caribou. I was on the British Columbia side then, and at the time that province allowed two caribou to the license. I could have shot him without moving from my tracks, but somehow I preferred seeing him run.

During the madness of the love-making moon, caribou do some very odd things indeed. The bulls particularly are subject to aimless runs, and often in glassing for game, the hunter will see a big bull all alone traveling from nowhere to someplace else.

When the rut really gets under way, the hopeful and myopic eyes of the amorous bulls turn everything into cow caribou, and a couple of times I have been put afoot when lovelorn caribou ran my horse off. One time up on the St. Claire in the western Yukon, I saddled a horse and took off alone to ride as far as I could up the side of a mountain. I then tied my horse to some willows and started on foot toward the crest in order to glass the basins on the far side.

I had hardly got going when I noticed a small bunch of caribou about half a mile away—a young bull, a couple of cows, and two calves. Paying no further attention to them, I completed my climb and lay down to use my binoculars. I was engrossed in my task when I heard hoofs pounding behind me, and I looked up to find that the whole bunch of caribou had followed me so they could get a good whiff and decide what I was. They would smell me, flee in panic, then forget what they had smelled, come back for another good sniff, then flee more. They simply couldn't figure out what I was doing lying there on the ground. Finally I lost patience with them, jumped up and let out a yell, and chased them off the mountain.

I found some ewes, lambs, and small rams in basins, but no big rams, so I decided to go back to my horse and ride to camp. But when I got to the spot where I'd tied him, he was gone. The reason? You've guessed it. That bunch of half-witted caribou had decided to investigate him. Their fresh tracks were all around. When I finally made my way laboriously back to camp through the muskegs and bug brush, the horse was there. The cook said that when he'd come in he had been running as if the devil were after him.

A couple of weeks later Field Johnson and I, taking a jack camp with two saddle horses and one packhorse, went clear to the glaciers at the head of the St. Claire. I shot two rams there. We packed our riding saddles with heads and sheep meat and started back for the main camp on Harris Creek, leading our horses. The packhorse followed.

Our poor old packhorse was pretty weary. He was heavily loaded, and for over a week he had been above timberline, deprived of his favorite pea vine and living on willow leaves. He dragged along, getting farther and farther behind, slogging along with his head down and wanting nothing except to get rid of his heavy pack and have a square meal.

The rut was in full swing then, and caribou were constantly in sight all around us. None of us paid any attention to them. Suddenly I heard the pounding of hoofs, and a big bull caribou dashed up to investigate Old Baldy, the packhorse. Baldy had never been so insulted in his life. His hind feet lashed out, and he caught that big bull right in the jaw with a crack that sounded like a rifle shot. Then he fled in one direction and the bull in the other. For the rest of our trek Baldy kept right behind us, and every time he'd see or smell a caribou he'd snort and roll his eyes.

The crowning glory of the caribou, and of most interest to the sportsman, is his wonderful rack, the largest antlers in proportion to body weight of any of the world's game animals.

All caribou antlers are built on the same pattern, and yet no two are just alike. The unique feature of all these antlers is the brow point, or snow shovel, which projects outward from the face. On the average caribou head, there is a shovel on one side and a spike on the other. Sometimes the shovel is only a few inches wide, but in the Yukon one time I shot a bull with a 17-inch shovel, and I've heard of some even wider. Those first seeing a caribou head always ask what the shovel is used for. It looks as if it would be useful for pushing snow away from the lichens on which caribou feed. Actually, it has no known use. Caribou generally paw to expose their feed, and they shed their antlers in midwinter when, if they used their shovels to push away snow, they would be the most useful.

Occasionally one sees a head with a double shovel, and these heads are greatly prized. I have already told how I was about to stalk one double-shovel bull in British Columbia only to have him get up and trot aimlessly off. The only other bull I have seen with a double shovel was in the Yukon. I was riding along a river bar and he got up out of some big brush in which he had been lying. When I piled off my horse and grabbed my rifle, he faded back into some scrubby black spruce and I did not see him again. He was then in the process of cleaning the velvet from his antlers. The job was about half done, and long streamers of velvet waved from his magnificent antlers like moss from a live oak.

In the Yukon the big bulls leave the country above timberline and go down into the first scrubby trees when the time comes to clean off the velvet. One day there will be no big bulls up on the barrens at all, and the next day they are all over, their horns bright and freshly cleaned.

Curving forward above the shovel on caribou antlers is the formation known as the "bez," and about halfway up the antlers a spike projects to the rear. The top portion of the antlers is generally palmated, and it is this wide palm, combined with the shovel, that makes the caribou head so handsome. Occasionally, though, this palmation is absent, and instead the top portion consists of a number of points.

Even a fair caribou head is quite a handsome trophy. A really big one is a grand sight indeed. I have seen the famous Pop head in Vancouver, B. C., the head that has for years been the No. 1 mountain caribou. The handsomest I have ever run into, though, is one from an animal shot by Elgin Gates, an old hunting companion of mine. It appears as No. 5 in the 1958 edition of *Records of North American Big Game*. The finest freshly taken head I have ever seen was the one my son Bradford got in the Cassiars in 1951. He won the Boone and Crockett Club award with it, and it was No. 5 in the 1952 record book, No. 12 in that of 1958.

Of all the places I have hunted caribou, I believe I have seen a higher percentage of outstanding heads among the great Osborn caribou in the Cassiar district of northwestern British Columbia. They average a good deal larger than the heads of the mountain caribou to the east and south, and in the record book almost all the big heads are from the Cassiar. The heads of the Barren Ground caribou shown in the record book average a bit larger, but I believe this is because more Barren Ground caribou are taken. Very few bulls of this type are killed in the Cassiar as compared with areas in Alaska and the Yukon where the bulk of Barren Ground caribou are found.

Caribou are restless wanderers. Some areas of suitable country always have caribou, but many sections of what looks like ideal caribou country have no caribou at all. Some of the wandering is from the winter to the summer range. Some of it may be drifting in front of storms, but much of this migration seems to be without reason. In 1956, when I was hunting white sheep around Prospector Mountain in the Yukon, we packed through great areas of fine looking caribou country. The herds had been there once, as we saw many old bleached heads, but all the time we were there we saw not a single animal, not even a single fresh track. We had to move into an entirely different area for caribou trophies. Indians tell me that a certain piece of country may be full of caribou for a few years and then suddenly the animals move away. No one knows why.

In many areas the caribou move from open country in the summer and early fall to the subarctic forests in the winter, as the trees break the blasts of the bitter boreal winds. Often in the summer, I am told, caribou run long distances upwind to get away from the torture of northern mosquitoes. Before the frosts kill the mosquitoes in early fall, the caribou can be seen standing on high ridges in the wind. With their dark bodies and light necks, they are colored much the same as Stone sheep, and are often found right in sheep country. But even at a range of several miles it's not difficult to tell a ram from a caribou, as the caribou always stand with their heads down.

Eskimos and Indians in caribou country kill great numbers of the animals, eat the flesh, make clothes and sleeping robes from the hides, and tools from the horns. I have been told that the Eskimos even eat the acid soaked caribou moss in the stomachs as a salad. The natives are not very numerous, but each family will kill great numbers of caribou annually. So will trappers and prospectors. It is no great trick to pile up 10 or 15 animals out of a herd.

The principal enemy of the caribou, however, is the big northern wolf. Probably the wolf is as necessary to the health and well-being of caribou herds as the cougar is to the well-being of the mule deer. Overgrazing is a far more serious enemy of any herbivorous animal than is predation. In Alaska there has been considerable wolf control by shooting from light airplanes and also by poisoning, and I understand that the caribou herds of Alaska are on the increase—so much so that some biologists are fearful that in some sections they are too plentiful for their food supply.

Reindeer from Norway were introduced into Alaska, by the government to help the economy of the Eskimos. For a time the reindeer increased spectacularly, and some Eskimos had herds of thousands. But in the long run the reindeer declined, and the experiment was pronounced a failure. Some have laid the blame on the Eskimos, saying that they would not take enough care of the deer and the animals were killed by wolves and driven off by the wild caribou. Biologists have told me, however, that the reason the experiment failed was that the reindeer became too plentiful, overgrazed the caribou moss and other forage plants, and died. The same thing could happen to the caribou if they were allowed to become too plentiful.

Residents of the Yukon tell me that the caribou are slowly declining, and I have read that the numbers are also going downhill in the Canadian arctic. There is very little wolf control in Canada, and natives hunt them hard.

For my part, I have never seen an area where caribou were too plentiful. Even on a 30-day trip around the head of the White River in the western Yukon, I seriously doubt if I saw 1,000 caribou—and I was in excellent caribou country all the time. When I was in the Pelly Mountains of the eastern Yukon in 1949, I found them very scarce, by no means plentiful in the Cassiar or Muskwa-Prophet River country of British Columbia, and only in good huntable numbers in the high mountains along the Alberta-British Columbia border.

As near as I can remember, I have shot 14 bull caribou in British Columbia, Alberta, and the Yukon. Unless my memory plays me false, I have shot two of these with the 180-grain bullet in the .30/06 and the rest with the 130-grain bullet in the .270. My impression is that the big, offbeat deer are quite easy to kill. One of the reasons, of course, is that they are generally found in open country and the hunter has plenty of time to make his shots count. The only caribou I have ever had any difficult killing was the very first bull I shot up in Alberta. He was something over 200 yards away and was trotting uphill broadside. I shot him three times through the lungs with the 130-grain Silvertip bullet from the .270 before he went down. He did not move out of his tracks after the first shot, but he took two others before he fell. This one experience made me believe for a few days that a bull caribou must be an animal of considerable vitality, but since that time no caribou I have hit has run over 30 paces, and most of them have gone down in their tracks with the first shot. In the far north the Eskimos who live on caribou prefer light cartridges like the .218 Bee, the .222, and the .22 Hornet for their caribou shooting, as they can carry a great deal of the light ammunition. Farther south the trappers and Indians use more .30/30's than anything else.

The best caribou I ever shot was taken in 1945 not far from Tepee Lake near the Alaska-Yukon border. I discovered a small bunch of caribou high on a ridge above camp and about three miles away. My guide, the late Johnny Johnson, and I decided to try for them in the morning.

When we got up it was a cold, dreary, overcast day. A little light, dry snow fell now and then, and all in all it looked like a fine day to sit in the cook tent by the stove drinking tea and telling stories.

But I couldn't get over those bulls on the skyline. A couple of them looked as if they had very good heads. So Johnny and I left camp, riding our horses to the base of the mountain and then climbing and leading. When we got on top, the place where we had seen the bulls was all tracked up, but no caribou did we see.

There were high, snow-covered peaks in every direction, and big empty basins. Below us we could see the little white tents of our camp and faintly hear the tinkle of the horse bells.

Clouds hung low, filling some of the basins with the gray, dirty-looking mist and clinging to the peaks in ragged streamers. We glassed in every direction, moved on, glassed again. We saw nothing. Below us a big basin was filled with fog so thick that it looked as though you could walk on it. We decided if the caribou were anywhere, they were in that basin. And so it proved. Little by little the fog below us began to break up and drift off, and finally, right in the middle of the basin and about a mile away, our binoculars showed us four fine bulls.

We got behind a fold in the ground and kept out of sight of the caribou as we dropped into the basin. Then, carefully watching the wind, we made a long circle. We finally came out about 400 yards from the bulls. Johnny wanted to get closer, but I told him I'd rather shoot at a standing caribou at 400 yards than a running caribou at 300. I had plenty of time, so I lay down on a low ridge and got into a tight sling. Holding high to allow for the two-foot drop, I squeezed my first shot off at what looked like the best bull. He ran in a little circle and fell. The others slowly trotted off. Holding high and swinging well ahead, I shot again, and the second one I had picked went down in his tracks.

The best bull of the two is in the record book for the Barren Ground caribou, and the antlers of the second have massive top portions and one of the widest shovels I have even seen on a caribou head. The other two bulls trotted off about half a mile and then stood watching as Johnny and I took off the heads and capes and gutted the animals so we could come back the next day for the meat. Afraid that wolves, foxes, or bears might chew up the heads during the night, Johnny and I decided to carry them out to our horses, and on the way we stalked and shot a grizzly. Quite a day!

I don't suppose a story on the caribou would be complete without something about the meat. Like that of almost any other animal, it is excellent in late summer and very early fall just before the rut—tender, juicy, and full of flavor. Once the rut starts, though, it quickly takes on a taste which to me seems like that of the strongest domestic mutton. I do not particularly care for it then, but it never gets foul, in my experience, as does the flesh of a rutting bull moose.

Like most rutting males, bull caribou eat little if anything during the rut, and their flesh quickly becomes dry. While they are losing weight, the hard, firm fat on their backs has seemed to me to become foamy. After the rut they lose their strong taste, according to the late Jean Jacquot, dean of the Yukon outfitters. He told me that winter caribou meat is the best "poor" meat in the arctic.

Near-sighted, jittery, not very bright, the caribou is nevertheless perfectly adapted to his environment, and a handsome addition to anyone's trophy room.

Outdoor Life, July 1960

A Dream Trophy

BY GRANCEL FITZ

But it was a planned dream, this biggest Newfoundland caribou in 10 years, even if I did nearly spoil it all.

In the cabin on Deer Lake that served as a base for Ray Wellon's bush airplanes, we unfolded my big map of Newfoundland. I had outlined four small areas on it in pencil. Fairly well separated, they were deep in the southern interior, and I pointed to a remote patch that scaled out to roughly 15 miles wide.

"That's where we want to go," I told Gene Manion, who would fly the little plane. "If it doesn't pan out in a couple of days, we'll try one of the others."

"I figure we'll get there in about two hours," Gene said.

The plane was loaded with our simple camp gear, and its pontoons left the water a few minutes later to carry us eastward in the bright sunshine of an early October day. In only a few minutes, we were crossing the narrow expanse of Grand Lake, and soon we were speeding over the Rainy Lake country where Wellon has a hunting camp.

"From all accounts, they've seen a caribou with a real big rack around there," Gene remarked to me.

Only the evening before, I'd been told about this giant bull by a hunter who saw it after filling his license with a handsome, 30-point trophy that wasn't quite big enough for the official records. A somewhat bigger specimen than his was just what I wanted. But, on assignment from *Outdoor Life*, I was following a very special plan, and I wasn't going to try my luck in the Rainy Lake region if I could help it.

We flew onward over countless brooks, puddles, ponds, and larger lakes. In contrast with the mountain scenery we had left in the lower Humber River valley, there were only occasional, isolated hills. The farther we went, the more open and barren the country became. Somewhere beyond Red Indian Lake we noted a few small, scattered groups of little white dots. These were the first Newfoundland caribou I had seen, and the total came to around 25 before we crossed that locality and entered a broad strip that seemed completely empty.

"The area you marked is just ahead," Gene said at last.

I soon realized that the choice of landing places would be limited. Very few of the nameless ponds were big enough to let us take off from them safely, but Gene brought us down on a larger one— scarcely 50 yards long—and dodged rocks in taxiing to its northern edge. There he tied the plane in the shelter of the bank.

"Here's a place we can pitch the tent," he said.

I scrambled ashore. He had found a level spot not far from the water's edge. But we could make camp later. I was anxious to hunt while the weather was good, having learned how quickly it can change. Soon we started out through an open and fairly wide corridor covered with yellow marsh grass that stretched away to the west between stands of spruce.

Once or twice we had to detour some soft spots, but none of the footing could match the really treacherous muskeg in parts of northern British Columbia and various ranges of the Barren Ground caribou. Stretches of tundra covered with hummocks of typical caribou moss were less common here; they often gave way to grassy bogs and to firmer ground carpeted with a kind of short buckbrush. Most of the forested sections, which had seemed to be trifling when we flew over them, now proved to be considerably bigger.

Perhaps a mile from the plane, the edge of the timber on our right curved back sharply, and when we passed that point we saw a bull caribou lying in some buck brush about 150 yards away. His antlers were so tall they startled me. Gene and I froze in our tracks. The gentle north wind blew directly toward where we stood and I was glad the bull hadn't spotted us as I raised my binoculars for careful look at him. With more features to consider than on any other antlered animal, caribou heads aren't easy to judge in a hurry.

This one showed four or five top points on each side—not big, but acceptable for a woodland specimen. His slender main beams were straighter than most, and therefore were shorter than their height suggested. They would tape a bit more than 40 inches. His double brow palms were rather small, and he had about 30 antler points, all told. His most remarkable features were his extremely long second, or bez, points. They curved far out to their high-carried end palms, which weren't much wider than my hand. That length would count heavily in an official trophy score.

"The head looks light," Gene commented, summing up a major weakness.

"I wish he'd face this way and show me his spread," I said.

Seemingly eager to oblige, the bull stood up. So did a cow that had been bedded near him in the low brush. The bull was the biggest-bodied woodland specimen I've ever looked over. The hair on his gleaming snow-white neck was so long and thick that it hung in an enormous dewlap. His fine spread of antlers almost equalled their length, and after some quick calculations I decided that he could make the lower brackets of the record class. But the spindly conformation of his rack bothered me, and I knew that he wouldn't do for my collection.

"He'd make the record book," I told Gene, "but I'm going to pass him up."

Turning from temptation with the thought that our hunt had hardly begun, we continued walking. And those curious caribou came right along, narrowing the distance between us. We stopped. They stopped. We went on, speeding up and angling somewhat away from the wind to discourage their notion of circling in front to get our scent. That, I knew, would start them racing off into country where they might spook a finer trophy. But they kept abreast, and soon we were barely 60 yards apart.

"Go back where you came from, you old fathead," I said to the bull.

While I doubt he understood me, he proved again that he aimed to please by ceasing to follow when we moved off. Before long he was heading toward where we had found him, taking with him the one bride he had so far collected.

The rest of the day turned up no other notable heads, but enough ordinary caribou to keep things interesting. We were careful to avoid giving any of them our scent. One young bull and a couple of cows waited until we were within 50 yards. They they walked on ahead of us exactly like driven cattle.

When we finally went back to organize our little camp, I had sized Gene up as a smart outdoorsman who knew his hunting as well as his airplanes, and he had surely proved himself to be an excellent companion. My greatest satisfaction, however, was in the behavior of the caribou we'd found. This reinforced my confidence in the plan I had carefully worked out. That plan, which has possibilities in other regions, was designed to answer a challenge that differed drastically from any other I had ever tried to meet.

In 1959, when I'd finally collected all 25 legal, big-game animals in North America, it seemed reasonable to limit my future hunting on this continent to the nine classes in which I had never bagged an officially listed, record-class specimen. In two classes particularly—woodland caribou and Columbian blacktail deer—the best examples I'd shot were nothing to be proud of. But when I thought of trying for a really outstanding woodland caribou last fall, the prospects seemed downright discouraging.

Newfoundland is the traditional hunting ground which has produced the finest heads in the past. Four from there were recorded in 1951. None of these was equalled by any of the five that turned up since, however, and neither the number nor the quality of those taken after 1955 warranted a class in later Boone and Crockett Club competitions. Newfoundland it had to be, though. Besides, no other Canadian province has had an open woodland caribou season in many years.

How good a chance did Newfoundland offer? I had never been there. Although I'd had considerable experience with other caribou races, my only encounters with the woodland species had been in northern Quebec and in Saskatchewan, where I'd run across them while hunting other game. I also knew that quite a number of keen trophy hunters had gone to Newfoundland in recent seasons and failed to find a decent head. At the same time, many men who weren't so choosy had successful hunts. Since the population of ordinary caribou seemed sufficient, there had to be at least a few big ones. And with Canada's long tradition of catering to visiting sportsmen, there had to be some good guides too. I began to wonder why trophy racks were so rarely brought out.

A little investigation clarified the picture. Several hunters reported that, while the outfitting in most cases had been excellent, the kind of footing in the caribou-bogs made it hard to cover much ground. The outfitters had a different story. They felt that too many sportsmen were either unwilling or unable to walk far enough to find trophy heads and preferred to hang around camp.

Both viewpoints made sense, but I knew that among the unlucky trophy hunters were some serious and thoroughly able-bodied veterans. If the record-class trophies were so seldom close enough to camp for them to reach, what were my chances of doing better? Here was a challenge I'd have to lick with my head instead of my legs, and before long I came up with a theory.

There was every reason to believe that the best hunting camps had been located—some of them many years ago—in the centers of excellent game regions. Knowing that many of their clients liked to be pampered, the prominent, long-established outfitters made their camps uncommonly comfortable. After that, it was only natural for them to take their dudes to the same places year after year. When a region which must be covered on foot from a central base is pounded to that extent, the heads to be found there can hardly be other than ordinary ones.

At that point I was ready to apply the theory I've used for 30 years. This is that fine trophies can be taken if the hunter goes to the right place at the right time with the right guide, and then keeps hunting hard and passing up the smaller specimens until the real prize shows up. Naturally, plenty of advance research is often needed to satisfy the first three requirements, and either the hunter or his guide must know how to judge heads.

The ideal place for heads that hadn't been picked over would be a rutting area for caribou that had not been hunted in recent years. Suggestions from guides or from other sportsmen would be of no help; I didn't want to go where they had been. But if I went to Newfoundland a few days before my hunting began, I might find somebody who could give me solid information.

Experience with other kinds of caribou provided me with most of the answers about when to hunt. The rutting time for all of them starts in early October. In Newfoundland—where the 1960 open season would run from September 12 to October 29—a man after venison along with his trophy head should hunt during the first week or 10 days. Later he'd run into a peculiar situation. Many trophy specimens of elk, moose, or deer furnish good meat at the height of the rut—even though this is hardly the time to expect it at its best—but a rutting bull caribou simply isn't fit to eat.

On the other hand, early season is a bad bet for getting top-flight heads. The older bulls are then spending too many daylight hours in the dense evergreen forests where they are hard to find. There's not much chance of inspecting many racks before the animals come out into the open barrens, usually in the first week in October. From that time on there may be other problems. Some of the many small points on caribou antlers are often broken as soon as the rutting battles get underway, and plenty of trophy heads are practically ruined.

Also, the heavy frosts that must come before the rut really gets going may be followed, all too quickly, by enough of a general freeze-up to make it hard to get out of the country. Not much ice is needed to prevent a pontoon-equipped plane from taking off.

Finding the right guide in Newfoundland didn't seem too important. Although the law sensibly requires a nonresident sportsman to be accompanied by a licensed guide, I was planning my 55th hunting trip for big game and felt qualified to size up a caribou rack and stalk the animal without any help. I wasn't worried about getting lost, either. What I really needed was a competent bush pilot to fly me to a place I'd select for myself. I also wanted him to stay with me until my hunting was over so I could change my territory or pull out promptly if the freeze-up threatened.

This approach was tempting, and on September 28 I began to organize things in St. John's, the provincial capital. Crossing the whole island from west to east to get there had already given me some idea of the country. As I didn't know where I'd end up, Trans Canada Air Lines solved the travel problem. My return ticket would let me stop off at the airport nearest my hunting grounds—when I decided where they would be.

From the air, the Newfoundland landscape seems to belong much farther north than it actually is. Here is caribou country that was world famous before I was born. Remembering my own first canoe trip in the north, I could imagine how hard it had been for old-time sportsmen to get around in it, or even to get there at all. The speed and comfort of the Viscount plane made me realize how fast the world has changed.

Through the Canadian Government Travel Bureau in New York, I'd learned of a bush plane contact. The Newfoundland Tourist Development Office in St. John's had furnished the original information, so I made my first stop there. They told me that Wellon's Flying Service, outside the city of Corner Brook on the west side of the island, had the kind of planes I wanted. I was informed that Ray Wellon also was an outfitter and could get me a guide. Next, in the Department of Mines and Resources, I met Stuart Peters, the Deputy Minister, and A.T. Bergerud, the game biologist. Both of these young scientists are well informed, and they brought me up to date on the caribou situation.

"A mysterious malady has been killing off newborn calves for the last several years," Peters said. "This season, we are issuing only 200 caribou licenses. We're now encouraging the moose hunters."

With 45,000 moose in flourishing shape, Newfoundland has turned into a moose country. The bag limit is now three to a hunter in one zone.

After I'd learned that not more than 5,000 caribou were left in all Newfoundland—with only about 800 mature bulls—I wondered whether I was justified in hunting them at all. But I soon realized that the present game management program is in good hands, and that taking out less than 200 old trophy bulls would have no effect on the species.

My first three days in St. John's were mainly spent in considering areas which had no hunters but might have some good caribou. The three zones open for hunting them took in roughly a third of the island's 43,000 square miles. Assuming that only 100 of the 800 known mature bulls carried heads good enough to suit me, each of them would have an average of about 140 square miles to get lost in—one good reason why so few were taken. There were, however, areas that had none.

After gathering suggestions from all sources I could think of, I got a big map of the whole island and a series of inch-to-the-mile government maps covering the sections that seemed most promising. When I'd studied these in relation to what I'd learned about caribou habitat in other areas, I made my final choice and caught a plane to Stephenville on October 1.

A 60-mile taxi ride took me to Corner Brook. From there, I promptly moved into the night club Ray Wellon runs, along with his other activities, six miles out of town on the Humber River. It was closer to his Deer Lake airplane base, and the accommodations were very comfortable. Like everyone else I met on this trip, Ray did all he could for me. It developed that Gene Manion, one of his pilots, was also a qualified guide, so I was all set. There was only one trouble. My plan called for hunting after a hard frost signaled the start of the rut. The weather, however, was much too warm. And having got this far, I was determined to carry out my campaign as perfectly as possible.

The break finally came on October 5—and that brings us back to the Deer Lake cabin and my first day's hunting.

Early on the morning of our second day, as Gene and I were getting ready for breakfast, I saw a small-headed bull caribou on the sparsely timbered ridge behind camp. One cow kept him company. A light breeze came from the north, toward the lake as on the day before, so they couldn't get our wind. Not much more than 100 yards away, these unexpected visitors watched us until we were almost ready to leave.

"Now the caribou have started hunting us," Gene said. "Maybe it's a lucky sign."

We headed again to the west, and finally a big, solitary bull showed himself in the early afternoon. His lack of female attendants was soon explained. From the trophy standpoint, his right antler was excellent, but the heavy main beam of his left one had been broken off just above the bez branch. It must have taken a terrific smash to do that. This old fellow proved that some of the serious fighting had begun.

He seemed little concerned with us, although we were in a bog with no cover. I wondered if I could stalk close enough to get a really good picture of him. Then the fun began, because this sort of thing calls for the type of telephoto equipment which is too bulky to pack when you are hunting in earnest with a rifle. I wanted to get within 30 yards. The bull wouldn't let me, but he stayed close enough to keep me trying. As our slow and patient game game went on, he led the way into some country we might not have otherwise explored. And there, in a shallow open basin, I spotted a bewildering number of caribou in a single herd. We settled down to do a thorough job with our binoculars.

The animals were 600 or 700 yards away, and we counted 18 after doing our best to search out all the less conspicuous ones. I checked them over several times before I was satisfied there was only a single bull. Bearing in mind that woodland caribou have short, compact antlers—the minimum record-class score for them is 295 points, compared with 350 for the mountain and Barren Ground groups—I saw that he had a heavy and huge-framed rack with fine brow palms and broad bez palmations. His main beams swept away back before curving forward, and I felt sure they were close to 45 inches long. He also had at least a 40-inch spread. The number, length, and palmation of points near the beam ends would have to be studied at closer range, for they meant a lot in the trophy ranking. It is in this top development, often so spectacular on heads of the other classes, that most woodland specimens fall down. If his tops turned out to be even moderately good, this bull would surely satisfy me.

The puzzling part was the size of this sultan's harem. Woodland caribou at that time of year are normally split up into small rutting companies in which individual bulls have rarely gathered as many as a dozen cows. All at once I thought of an answer.

"Gene," I said, "I'll bet this so-and-so broke the antler off our playmate and stole all his gal friends."

"Could be," he agreed. "He looks big enough to do it. How do you plan to stalk him?"

The question didn't have an easy answer. Caribou may be simply uneducated. More likely, however, these gorgeous beasts are probably just plain stupid. While deer, elk, and moose have learned to thrive close to civilization, caribou are often said to avoid all contact with man by migrating away from him. I wonder. Most of them, I think, have migrated to the great beyond after having been too curious about natives with rifles.

In any case, most caribou believe nothing but their noses. Unless you've alarmed them, you can nearly always walk up for a 200-yard shot with no careful stalking whatever when the wind is in your favor. But you cannot count on this invariably. So I don't like to take chances with an outstanding trophy, and with nothing in the muskeg to conceal us I didn't want to go directly toward this bull. Here, as we faced the herd, the wind blew straight across from right to left. The terrain just beyond the caribou showed a series of bare little ridges. These would offer some cover if we approached from the far side. We could get there unseen if we moved to our left and traveled in the timber which almost encircled the whole open space.

First, we had to get rid of the bull with the broken antler. That was managed when I led the way into the woods and stopped. After crossing in front of us, he came back to where he caught our scent and then promptly romped off into the forest. Things went smoothly from that point on. The herd was out of sight. In less than an hour we were almost opposite our starting place and ready to move into the open across those grassy ridges toward where the caribou had been. As they were on their feet and feeding when we saw them last, I thought they had probably moved just a little.

A few minutes later, easing up one ridge with Gene a couple of steps behind me, I looked over its top and spotted a cow lying down on the farther slope of the little dip between us. The wind, of course, was now coming from our left. This harem inmate was to the right of a line from us to where I thought the sultan himself might be. If I kept going ahead, she would surely scent me. To make things worse, I saw another cow in the draw below her.

What to do? When we were in the timber, apparently, the herd had drifted over to lie down among the ridges. The bull might now be quite close. If we backed away from the two cows to pass them on the downwind side, we would sacrifice the concealment the rolling terrain had given us. And if we alarmed them before the bull was in sight, the same ridges could easily cover his escape.

"I'm going a short way to the left, then straight on in," I told Gene. "Those cows are bound to smell us, but I'm gambling on finding the bull before they mess things up."

This route took us to a bit higher ground. We looked over the nearer ridge to the one beyond it, and there we saw the tops of a pair of antlers. In a moment they slowly disappeared behind the crest. The tops were the only features of the bull's head I hadn't checked earlier but on this occasion there'd been time to count four passably good points near the end of each beam. Added to the excellence of his other qualities, they were enough. From the nearer ridge, the range would be about 200 yards. With never a doubt that a splendid head was mine for the taking, I went ahead for the kill.

When I crossed the hollow, those downwind cows got to their feet and started to go. Hastening up the little slope, I knew I had to concentrate on placing my first bullet exactly, for there might be no second shot if the bull ducked behind the ridge. Fortunately, I wouldn't have to worry about his head any longer, for I knew all about that.

There he was! As he neared the top and turned almost broadside, I could even see his knees. I sat down. The scope-sight picket of my old Griffin & Howe .30/06 steadied on his shoulder, and when Gene came up to where he also saw that caribou, I was starting a careful trigger squeeze.

In that instant, Gene said, "Wait!"

May I never forget the lesson of the next few seconds. I had been a complete jackass, and only Gene's timely word had saved me from filling my license with a nice, better-than-average bull I didn't want. Looking at the whole animal, Gene had known instantly that it wasn't the sultan we had seen before. This one, with the tops I'd checked, carried a different head in all other respects. I hadn't even glanced at it. My attention had been focused on the animal's shoulder. Stupid as it may seem, the possibility of a second bull in this part of the basin had never occurred to me. So I felt deeply grateful.

We pushed ahead then and promptly learned that the cows we'd scared belonged to the bull I'd almost shot. The big sultan and his large harem were still upwind. They had trotted off when we spooked the others, but they soon doubled back and stopped within easy rifle range to look at us. No longer trigger happy, I saw that while this bull's massive rack would measure just about what I'd thought, he carried only a single top point on each antler. He wouldn't do.

After we'd roamed around a little more, it was time to head for camp. As we trudged across the muskegs and worked through some strips of tangled forest, I felt let down. Thinking again of how few record-class, Newfoundland trophies the recent seasons had produced, I may have been beginning to wonder about the huge bull I'd passed up the day before.

We were within half a mile of the tent, marching through some open marshland with Gene a step or two ahead of me, when he stopped. He'd spotted a bull caribou and four or five cows near the edge of the timber to our left.

"Not as wide a spread as some of the others," he noted. "How does he look to you?"

The low sun was behind us as I raised the binoculars, then quickly lowered them.

"This hunt is over," I said.

ROUGH MEASURING. Official taping is done after 60 days.

I had seen a pair of fantastic bez palms and a rack with a whole forest of points. Its other features were too good to need study. As the bull wasn't more than 175 yards away, there was no reason to go closer. He was facing me squarely. Wanting no bloodstains on his beautiful white neck, I waited just long enough for him to turn a trifle and then squeezed off a 180-grain Silvertip. Although this sharply angled body shot would have been quickly fatal, it didn't knock him over. An instant later, when he turned a bit more, I finished him with another shot.

My excitement grew with every step toward the downed animal. I'd wanted a trophy that typified the classic woodland characteristics, and here was a dream head in that respect. When we had counted 42 antler points, it hardly disturbed me to note that he'd broken off a couple of other ones.

The more I examined him, the more delighted I felt. He would mark the 17th different North American species represented by a record-class head in my collection. Much later, in New York, I learned that he'd cinch eighth place in the present record list, and it was clear that this was the finest Newfoundland trophy since 1951. With Gene's help, I'd come up with a proper caribou instead of a boo-boo.

Outdoor Life, March 1961

Old Ephraim Country

BY CHARLES ELLIOTT

The legendary grizzly eluded us, but this was my finest bear hunt in many moons.

ook," I said, "I've just spent twelve bucks for a Wyoming nonresident fishing license, and so far I've only made a dozen casts. That's a dollar a throw. Wait until I've got my money's worth."

"Suits me," Roy Glasgow said, shrugging. "But something big has sure been working that cow over. He turned the bait completely around, and it takes a monster of a bear to do that. He also threw a scoopful of dirt over the carcass. Looks like a silvertip—maybe Old Eph himself."

"Eph?" I asked.

"Ephraim," Roy elaborated. "We've called him that around here for years."

He couldn't have said anything better calculated to get me out of the fishing business.

At that point, two other anglers, who had been fishing a big pool on the Clarks Fork River, came up. One of them, Gabby Barrus, does a daily stint for the Husky Oil Company in Cody and in the fall performs as a big-game guide. He also has published a number of stories on hunting and fishing. The other angler was Mike Miller, who owns and operates the K Bar Z Ranch on Crandall Creek in northwest Wyoming, where I was enjoying a fishing and hunting trip in late June of this year.

When Roy repeated his report, Gabby and Mike needed no arm-twisting either.

"No reason to take horses," Mike said. "The old logging road in there is rough as a cob, but we can drive to within four or five hundred yards of the spot."

While we bounced over the rugged terrain to the ranch, Mike filled me in on the bear situation in those parts.

"According to the game department," he said, "this area has more bears than any other in Wyoming, except maybe Yellowstone Park. Last spring almost every hunter who came out here filled his wife's order for a bear rug. Everett Wallace, the other outfitter, and I accounted for about thirty kills."

"How many grizzlies?" I asked.

"We try to concentrate on the troublemakers," Mike explained. "We may take one or two a year."

From the Game and Fish Commission, I later learned that there may not be an open season on grizzlies in 1968 in Wyoming, but even if there is, it will be on a limited-permit basis in certain areas.

At the ranch, Gabby and I swapped our fishing gear for rifles and warmer clothes; the ridgetops get mighty cold at twilight. I had my Kennon-built .300 Magnum and a variable Bausch & Lomb Balvar 8A scope. Gabby's bear medicine was a Model 99 .300 Savage—a lever-action rifle with open sights.

We drove up the soggy logging road that angled from the Forest Service station on Crandall Creek into the high country above Lodgepole Creek. The middle of the afternoon found us on a knoll overlooking the high park in which Roy had found bear sign.

Through Gabby's 7 x 35 Triton glasses, I looked at the remains of that old cow. She had died of natural causes, and the rancher had given the carcass to Mike for bear bait.

The bear was a big one, no doubt about it. The cow had been moved around as though it were a calf, and Roy, who had watched the bait almost daily since he and Mike had dragged it into the park, declared that whatever was eating on it had cleaned up more than half of the animal in two feedings.

After looking the park over from the hilltop, we settled down to wait under a gnarled spruce tree below the crest. For a couple of hours I shifted around on the rooty, rocky ground, trying to find a soft spot. I was beginning to wish I had brought a cushion along when a lightning-and-thunder storm began to drench the mountain. Standing up to get into our rain gear was a relief.

The storm passed, and I inquired in a whisper whether the wind, which was fishtailing from northwest to west and blowing our scent out across the park, wouldn't spook anything that came that way.

"It apparently doesn't," Mike said. "This is a good ridge for elk in the fall, and I've been parked under this very tree with the wind on my neck while elk fed all over the place. They don't seem to mind."

I must have looked dubious, for Roy said quietly, "There's a cow elk on the other side of the clearing now. The wind is from us to her, and if she caught our scent, she'd head out of this country like a turpentined cat." The elk was grazing and moving around, showing no interest in us.

"I'd guess," Mike said, "that the wind currents coming up this hill blow off into space when they top out."

I was watching through binoculars when the elk suddenly stopped grazing, did a little dance, stared over her shoulder, and then ducked into the timber.

Mike touched my arm.

"Don't move. There's a big bear coming into the open under the brow of the hill."

Without turning my head, I cut my eyes over to Roy and could see a look of disappointment on his face.

"Dern it!" he said under his breath. "Why couldn't he be Old Eph?"

A huge black—one of the largest I had seen in many a hunting moon—ambled into plain view through the sage, heading straight for the remains of the cow. Occasionally the black paused to look behind or in our direction before continuing along in that shuffling gait peculiar to all bears.

Then it stopped about 200 yards away and stared toward us for a full minute.

"He's not looking at us," Mike said. "He's just trying to see if the rest of his meal has been disturbed."

"He's a big one," Gabby said to me. "Think we ought to take him?

215

It's an easy shot."

I didn't know how to reply to that. I wanted a grizzly. Yet my license allowed two bears, and this was only the first day.

"He might be good insurance," I said.

"Wait until he gets on the carcass," Mike suggested. "Then you can decide."

The bear turned at an angle as if intending to circle and approach the cow from the other side. Then he shuffled on across the park, pausing frequently to look back toward the bait.

"He's not ready to feed yet," Roy whispered.

"I'm not going anywhere," I said.

We spent the next two hours watching the black. He grazed awhile in the meadow, then sat up on his rump and looked around. He dug for rodents or grubs and then chased something real or imaginary in a short circle through the edge of the woods.

We expected him to walk to the cow any minute, but he never again came any closer to us than 300 yards. I could have tried a shot at that distance, but I didn't feel we were that desperate for a kill. Just before dark, the bear shuffled across the upper end of the park and disappeared into the patch of woods out of which he had come. Roy swore under his breath.

"He'll probably go back to a bed he's got somewhere down in that thicket," Roy said, "and feed first thing in the morning. We should be here at daylight."

Mike had thrown a small tent into the back of his four-wheel-drive vehicle, and he put that up for Gabby and me. He and Roy rolled out their sleeping bags under the trees. We made coffee, ate a sandwich, and stretched out on the ground to wait for daylight.

Next morning we sat over the bait from first light at 4:45 until 9 o'clock, waiting for the black to show up. The time wasn't wasted, for we enjoyed watching a couple of deer, several elk, and a coyote.

The coyote cautiously circled the bait for half an hour but was never able to work up enough courage to take a bite out of food that smelled so strongly of bear.

It was during this morning watch that I got the lowdown on Old Ephraim from Roy Glasgow. I'd known Roy for many years and ranked him among the top Western guides. I can imagine him as one of the explorers or trappers of a century and a half ago who were woods-wise enough to keep their scalps in a country full of cantankerous Indians and short-tempered silvertips.

There wasn't a broken twig, bent blade of grass, or mark on the earth that Roy did not observe or could not interpret. He had the patience of a frontier mountain man; if he saw a movement in the forest, he would sit or stand motionless until he knew what it meant.

It was Roy, readers may remember, who was surprised by a grizzly and two cubs on a high ridge in sheep country a few years ago (see "This Happened To Me!" *Outdoor Life*, May 1962).

He had no gun, and when the silvertip charged him with her mouth open, he shoved his binoculars down her throat. Roy and the bear rolled down a slope, and the female grizzly clamped down on his leg. Roy's heavy leather chaps, plus a couple of cartridges and a cigarette lighter in his pocket, prevented her from biting all the way through. She finally threw him down a rock slide and went off after her cubs.

It took a modern contrivance to do what the wilderness, including grizzly bears, could not do. In August of this year, Gabby Barrus wrote me that Roy was dead. He had jacked up his car and was changing one of the shock absorbers when the jack slipped and the car fell on him.

Roy had known Old Ephraim for many years.

"Why did you name him that?" I asked.

"That's the name mountain men have always given to big silvertips," he replied.

Roy said the bear had a range of some 200 square miles. From time to time, lookouts on fire towers spotted him crossing a distant peak, and sometimes local cowmen saw him on a high slope or found his sign where he had dug for rock chucks on a sidehill.

One rancher found a half-eaten elk that had been wounded by a hunter the previous fall and had died in the high forest. The elk was covered with brush—sure sign of a grizzly—and while the rancher was examining the elk, Old Ephraim got out of his bed less than 100 feet away. He looked the rancher over, growled, and ambled almost nonchalantly into the forest.

The spring before, Mike and Roy had found grizzly tracks near a carcass and had brought one of their hunters up for the kill. They had been there only an hour when a fair-size black showed up and circled the dead animal warily, as though afraid of the grizzly scent. When the black finally came within range, the hunter shot him.

The guides went back to the carcass later. Tracks showed that Old Eph had been there and had cleaned up what remained of the animal as well as the skinned carcass of the black shot by the hunter.

A little later another hunter, while sitting on a hillside above a bait put out for Old Ephraim, suddenly had the funny feeling that something was watching him. He turned, and there, less than 30 feet away, stood the big bear on its hind legs, watching him. The hunter jumped for his rifle, but the bear vanished.

"The only real chance I ever had at that grizzly," Roy said, "was last spring. We had a bait out, and this fellow, who was more anxious to kill a silvertip than any other man I ever met, was in the blind with me. It wasn't more than seventy yards from where we sat to the bait—an open shot across a park.

"We'd been there about three hours, and I guess the hunter dozed a bit. Anyway, he didn't see the bear come in. I'm sure it was Old Eph. I shook the fellow and pointed out the bear.

"He didn't say a word. With his gun in his hand, he crawled right out the back of that blind. I grabbed him by the leg.

"'Where you goin'?' I asked.

"'I don't want no truck with nothin' that looks like that,' he said and kept on crawling.

"I could have shot the bear myself, but there's no percentage in that for a guide. The grizzly saw or heard us because he stood up and growled. But he didn't spook; he just went back to his feeding."

For the next week, when not watching bear baits, we did a bit of fishing for rainbow, brown, brook, and cut-throat trout, and rode the high country on horseback. We saw two bears at a distance, but they were traveling, and we knew we could never get to them.

This country intrigued me as much as any I had seen in Wyoming, and I know that state as well as I know my home state of Georgia. More than 1,000 square miles of wilderness lie generally south of the Montana border and east of Yellowstone Park. Some ranches and a few summer cabins are located along the streams at lower elevations, but most of this high hinterland, from 7,000 to 12,000 feet in elevation, can be reached only by trail.

The peaks along Yellowstone's east wall soar to spectacular heights, and the recesses cradle parks of lush grass plus hundreds of icy streams, most of them unfished and teeming with trout.

You find few horse tracks in the back country to indicate that anyone was there before you, and discarded papers and cans are delightfully absent. About the only people who come through are rangers and wardens, and in the fall a few hunters.

In many years of Western hunting, I'd never seen so much game. The area reminded me of the Thorofare 25 years ago, when only two or three hunting outfitters operated there.

You may meet deer on the trail at any hour of the day, and in late afternoon you can sit on a high hillside and watch elk grazing in almost every park. The rims are heavily marked with sheep tracks, and every marsh and meadow has its quota of Shiras moose. You hear stories of mountain lions, though they are not plentiful, and there is talk that next year the season may be opened on mountain goats at the head of Line Creek. The song of the coyote is ever present at twilight.

During the summer season, Mike Miller makes a few packtrips over the high east wall of Yellowstone Park and into a remote section seen by fewer than one out of a million of the park's visitors. The fishing his parties find there stretches the imagination.

Mike's rates at the K Bar Z Ranch for spring bear hunts are $65 a day with a seven-day minimum. He says that to be assured of a good trophy a hunter should plan to stay no fewer than 10 days.

In Wyoming, the spring season for blacks and grizzlies usually runs from April 1 to June 30, though grizzlies may be protected in 1968. There's a bear season in the fall, too.

We'd been at the ranch a week when Bud Bennett, from Springfield, Illinois, came in. Bud has oil interests in the West but always takes time out for a go at bears. He told us that the previous year he had made several trips and shot at seven bears before he finally got one.

"All the rest were clean misses," he said, grinning, "and to tell the truth, I didn't mind much. It's the hunting I like."

Another bear was working the carcass on Lodgepole Ridge, and we turned that one over to Bud and Punch Johnson, one of the ranch hands.

Roy, Mike, Gabby, and I rode up Reef Creek to check a bait in one of the creek bottoms. That afternoon couldn't have been more miserable. A cold rain mixed generously with sleet and snow—in late June, no less—slanted through the woods.

We tied our horses in a clump of trees on a narrow bench. Roy built a fire there, nursing it with wet wood.

"It's too early to go back to the ranch," he said to me after our noon sandwich. "I reckon this is a sorry day even for bears, but you and Gabby might as well go down and look that bait over for a while, just to keep off any critter that might have a mind to eat on it."

Mike walked down with us. We picked the thickest clump of trees on a bench overlooking the creek bottom and made ourselves as comfortable as possible. Not a creature was stirring, not even a whisky jack.

"Only people," Mike said, "are crazy."

We stuck it out for three hours—sitting, standing, leaning against trees. Up to that time I had always thought that turkey hunting required more patience than any other kind.

I decided that we were in for a busted afternoon. Mike seemed to read my thoughts.

"We've got a three-hour ride over a sloppy trail, and I guess it would be best to get out of the timber before dark. Roy's ramrodding this outfit, so I'll walk up and talk it over with him before we move."

Gabby and I agreed to remain where we were until the decision was made. I hoped it would be soon. The rain was cold enough to have ice in it, the wind was on the backs of our necks, and I had a feeling that every animal on that mountain had us pinpointed.

Mike disappeared into the rain and mist. I removed the piece of inner tube I use to protect my rifle scope, found the glass clear, and snapped the rubber band back on.

Suddenly Gabby hit the dirt as though his feet had been knocked out from under him.

"There's a bear coming down the hill beyond the creek," he hissed.

I saw the bear before he finished the sentence. It wasn't the grizzly we had hoped for. It was not even as large as the first black we had passed up. But it was a good medium-size black bear with a brown coat. Through the glasses I could see that the pelt was thick and long, almost silky.

"What do you think?" Gabby whispered.

"We didn't take out that insurance the last time a bear showed," I said. "Why don't you take him?"

"You've got two tags," Gabby said. "You'll have one left for Old Ephraim if we run into him."

While this *sotto-voce* conversation was going on, the bear disappeared in a mass of timber across the creek, and I thought we had let another one get away. Then I spotted him wading the stream, far below where we had first seen him. He turned and came up the bank, and we watched him approach.

I suddenly realized that he'd soon be out of sight under the brow of the hill. We might not see him again.

I was almost too late. All I could see through my scope was a network of twigs and limbs. To line up on the bear, I stood on tiptoe. I put the crosshairs on what I thought was the proper spot and squeezed off a shot just as the animal was about to disappear.

The bear did a backflip, landed on his feet, running, and I knew I had missed. Gabby and I ran onto the brow of the hill to get another look, but the bear was in a thicket.

We studied the hillside for five minutes. Then the black decided to leave the trees and climb the slope at an angle.

I judged the range to be about 250 yards. This time I sat down and propped my elbows on my knees for a steady rest. The bear was only a dozen steps from heavy timber when I squeezed off a shot. He collapsed and rolled down the slope.

THE AUTHOR (right) admires his bear with Gabby.

The black hadn't been out of hibernation long and did not have a pound of fat on him. Judging by his teeth, the bear was an old one. Roy estimated that the animal would have weighed 300 to 350 pounds after summer feeding.

The next day Bud missed a shot at a bear on Lodgepole Ridge. He just shrugged it off.

"I think he does it on purpose," Mike said with a laugh. "It gives him an excuse to come back here and try again. He'll get one before the season is over."

We camped for a couple of days in Reef Creek Valley. When we weren't watching the bait, Gabby and I crawled around the high rims. We found abundant sheep sign, but the bighorns were somewhere else. We also spent hours glassing elk and deer in high parks, but we saw no bears.

After two days we concluded that our wood smoke and camp noises might be considered unhealthy signs by the bear population, so we walked back to the ranch.

Two days later Mike, Gabby, and I rode back up to Reef Creek and discovered that something had tried to carry off the half-ton chunk of bait. The bait was fastened to a tree with heavy wire, and the wire had been stretched tight. The bait was partly covered with dirt.

"I'm sure this was done by a grizzly," Mike said excitedly.

For seven hours—and through two rain-and-snow squalls—we sat half a mile above the valley, watching the opposite mountainside and what we could see of the timbered valley through the rain and snow.

It was after 6 p.m. when we made a long circle in the timber toward the bench that paralleled the creek. As we approached the line of trees bordering the open bench, Gabby, who was in the lead, went down on all fours and motioned to us to do the same.

"Something just moved across the creek," he said. "I couldn't see what it was."

We glassed the opposite slope thoroughly but in vain.

"Must have spooked him," Mike whispered, "or he's circling to look us over. Old silvertips will do that sometimes."

He grinned when I looked behind me. Then he advanced slowly to the rim, peered over, ducked, and crawled back to us.

"A black is feeding on the bait," he said. "I got only a quick look and couldn't tell how big he is."

Gabby and I went to the rim on our hands and knees. We had to look a long minute before we made out a black bear partly hidden by a clump of trees.

"He's about the size of the one I got," I whispered. "Be my guest."

At a distance of about 80 yards and using open, iron sights, Gabby broke the bear's neck. He's an old-timer at this business.

Time was running out on my hunt, but Mike was still certain that the bait on Reef Creek had been hit by a grizzly, so we rode back there. Bud had gone home, so Gabby and Punch Johnson took over the Lodgepole bait.

Mike and I arrived late in the afternoon and decided to sit it out until dark in spite of the dangerous night ride off the mountain that would follow.

We soon ran out of conversation and lapsed into silence. I was thinking of the warm ranch house and the hot meal Mike's wife Connie would have for us when Mike touched my arm. I followed his gaze and then did a double take. Moving toward the bait was a big grizzly. I flipped the cover off my sights.

"Good luck at last," I whispered.

"Don't look now," Mike said, "but there's bad luck right in that bear's tracks."

At the silvertip's heels swaggered two cubs, seemingly trying to imitate their mother's every movement.

"Ah well," I sighed, "almost good luck anyway."

We watched the sow and cubs feed on the carcass for half an hour while the light grew dimmer under the trees.

"Let's get out of here," Mike said at last. "She might decide to sashay down the creek, and we might meet up with her in the dark."

As we rode through the high forest and later felt our way down the dark, muddy trail, I kept thinking of Old Ephraim and wondering whether he had sired the two grizzly cubs that had kept mama's hide from gracing the floor of my den.

Perhaps it's just as well that the old man himself didn't show. He would have been the climax to the most dramatic hunt I've had in many a season. But the fact that he is still wandering through those lofty parks and forests is all the excuse a man needs to go back there again.

Outdoor Life, December 1967

Credits